K P Weaver

Copyright © 2022 K P Weaver

First published in Australia in 2021
by Making Magic Happen Academy

www.makingmagichappenacademy.com
www.karenmcdermott.com.au

All rights reserved. No part of this book may be used or reproduced by any means, graphic, electronic, or mechanical, including photocopying, recording, taping or by any information storage retrieval system without the written permission of the copyright owner except in the case of brief quotations embodied in critical articles and reviews.

Editor: Teena Raffa-Mulligan
Cover and interior design: Ida Jansson

National Library of Australia Cataloguing-in-Publication data:
The Gift in Gratitude/Making Magic Happen Academy
Success/Self-help

ISBN (sc): 978-0-6455205-8-3
ISBN (e): 978-0-6455205-9-0

Gratitude is an attitude that will always provide.

CONTENTS

Introduction — 7

The Gratitude Formula — 9
Why Gratitude? — 13
How Gratitude Can Serve You — 18
Gratitude and Money — 23
Gratitude or Resentment? — 27
Gratitude and Kindness — 31
The Science of Gratitude — 35
Passing the Baton — 39
Gratitude, Your Choice — 43
Gratitude and Your Vision. — 47
If You Want It, Be Grateful for It Now — 51
Grateful Parenting — 54
Grateful Relationships — 57
Happy Dance with Gratitude for Next Level Impact — 61
Gratitude in Business — 65
Being Grateful When You Don't Feel It — 69
Gratitude Affirmations — 72

Love-fuelled Gratitude	76
The Gratitude Joyride	80
Being the Change – the World Needs More Gratitude	85
Find Gratitude in Procrastination	89
Gratitude and Health.	92
Grateful Creativity	96
The No-fear Approach to Gratitude	100
Gratitude in motion stories	**105**
Amanda Gore	*107*
Joanna Hunter	*113*
Veronica Gallipo	*125*
Kevin Monroe	*135*
Tracey Regan	*143*

INTRODUCTION

There is a world around us that is beyond the surface comprehension of most people. To consciously access it we have to go deeply inward which is quite often outside of our comfort zone. But that is where the magic happens and so it is worth pursuing. There is a hack that we can use to tap into this other realm and that is by using gratitude.

We all know what gratitude is; we express it in our lives — or not — every day. We work with the universal laws every day but it is usually an unconscious interaction. When we have the courage to side step into the unknown and choose to open our heart and mind to becoming more familiar with the power of possibility, we can navigate the laws that govern all that is, ever was and ever will be.

In this book I will share the how and the why behind gratitude. How you can incorporate it into your life and why you need to think strategically when you are grateful by understanding that gratitude actions a reaction.

I will share my personal experiences of gratitude in motion and the results I gained because of my open-minded gratitude perspective. We also have some wonderful special guests who share gratitude in motion in their lives so that you can learn from them.

If you are ready to embrace the greatest gift that you can give to yourself and others, then prepare to open your mind and embrace what the pages of this book shares.

One thing is for sure, we will all have successes and failures when it comes to gratitude. We may forget to express gratitude and we may not be mindful enough to leverage gratitude to manifest our heart's desire in our future by being grateful for it now. These things don't come naturally, they are learned. You will learn in the pages of this book the honest truth about gratitude and what you can achieve in life by embracing this softer yet impactful approach to life.

THE GRATITUDE FORMULA

There is a formula to gratitude that is quite simple in its theory yet often complicated for many in its application. I have found that it is a mindset that allows for a rhythm that gives way to a habit of productive gratitude.

Gratitude + emotion + focused intentions + aligned action = a winning gratitude formula.

You can't lose when you tap into this high frequency energetic vibration.

Gratitude alone will get results but if you want to experience next level experiences you will first be in the energy of gratitude and allow the essence of the emotions you are feeling to ripple through you so that you are emitting a high energy frequency. It is at this point when you should navigate some energy into what you want to manifest in your future. Then when inspired thoughts and/or opportunities aligned with those intentions present themselves to you, you will know. If you have the courage to action them straight away you will achieve results higher than you can ever imagine.

GRATITUDE

Take a moment to think in your mind and feel in your heart what you are grateful for in your life. Even someone experiencing the direst existence has the opportunity to tap into gratitude with the fact that they are alive. If that is all you can muster it is still something to be grateful for and can be used as a catalyst to manifest great things in your life if you allow it to do so.

Being grateful is a wonderful virtue and also an amazing tool for positioning yourself where you want to be in the future. You need to be grateful now for whatever you wish to experience in your life in order to have it in your future. It is a beautiful cycle that when you allow it to flow will create bucket loads of magic in your life.

EMOTION

One of the best ways to regulate high vibrational emotions is to prioritise joy as much as possible.

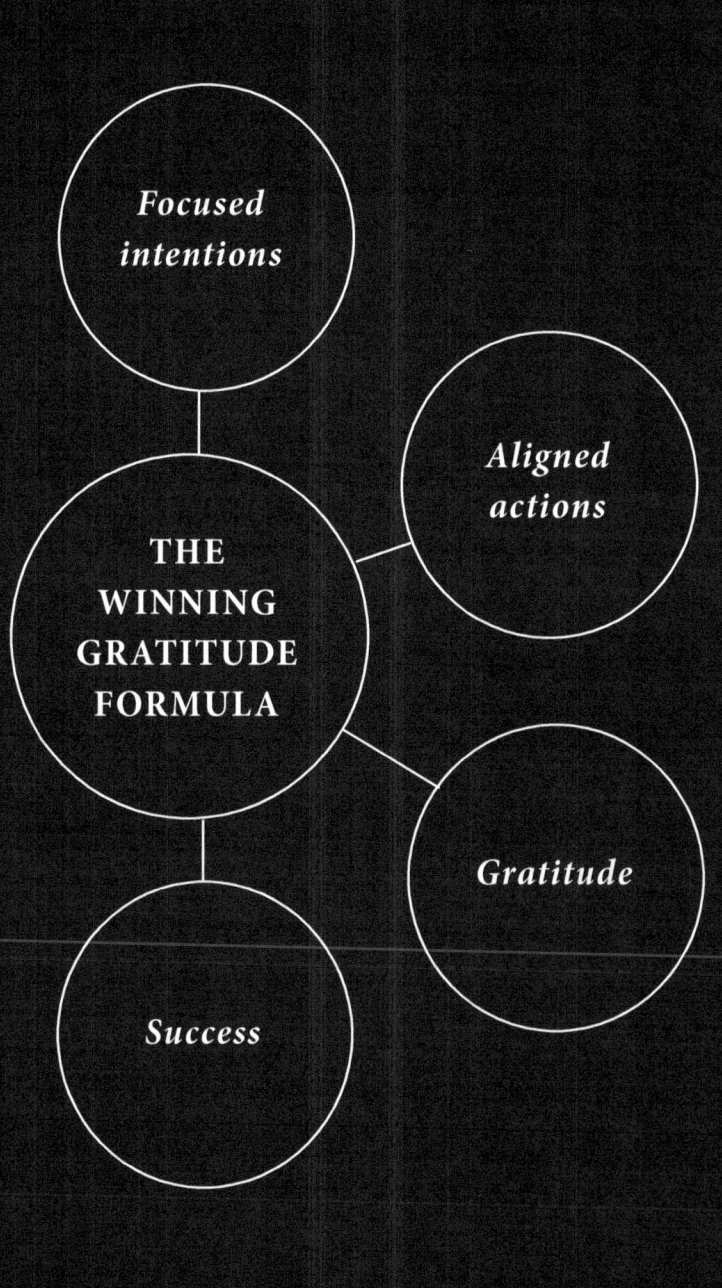

Super fuel your gratitude with a love for life and watch the results.

WHY GRATITUDE?

Gratitude is an instant hack into the flow of abundance. When you are grateful for something with all of your heart you can attract more of that goodness into your life. Most people do not understand the power of gratitude but the big thing here is that you don't need to understand it, you simply need to embrace it.

Over thinking things is a block to receiving. We need to allow things to be and trust that they are exactly as they need to be but of course, as humans we tend to overcomplicate things. It's in our genetics.

When I am asked, *why gratitude?* I reply, *why not?* Embrace gratitude and see the benefits you experience in your life.

I used to be one of those people who didn't value gratitude enough so I decided to be a test dummy and see what would happen if I became more grateful. Coming from a Catholic background I already knew how to say night-time prayers that were filled with gratitude, so I gave that a modern spin and sat in gratitude before I went to sleep every night. What was profound is that I instantly saw a difference in my life. Things became more positive from the get go. My relationship with my kids was much better and when I was grateful for the material things I had, I ended up with more. I knew it was to do with my new daily practice but I couldn't understand the logistics of it. The results were there so I decided to embrace it and so I say to you, don't overcomplicate things. Embrace this and the results will speak for themselves.

Ask yourself *why gratitude?* for you. What do you believe gratitude could bring into your daily life? Then prioritise it and watch the magic happen. Gratitude brings instant results into the lives of those who choose to see. As with everything in life, we need to choose gratitude every day. I have reaped the rewards for being steadfast with gratitude. Some days were easier than others but being mindful to be grateful every day was one of the best choices I have ever made. It had the power to turn what seemed to be a negative experience of life into a positive experience by helping me back on track after a dark period when I fell below the line and gratitude was not easy. But just because it wasn't easy didn't mean it was impossible, and each step towards gratitude took me a step further from the darkness. So whether you are investing in your mental wealth security deposit bank or trying to find your way out of the darkness, gratitude is a worthwhile investment every time! That is why you should choose gratitude!

An attitude of gratitude

Every action has an equal reaction so when you approach others and situations with an attitude of gratitude you can't lose.

Gratitude is a high vibrational choice. It's easy when reacting to an act of kindness but not so easy when it comes to actioning it without a catalyst, so choosing gratitude takes effort in the beginning. Some people have been brought up to be grateful through modems such as prayer and this is good practice but not the productive type of gratitude.

It keeps us humble and mindful of others and the small things in life. My issue with this is that it keeps us small, and the potential energy emitted from the gratitude we express is not channelled into our dreams so that we can make great things happen in our lives.

We need to have an attitude of gratitude that serves us because in doing so it will ripple out to our families, communities, and the world. The ripple effect of gratitude is always rooted in goodness, and we need more of that!

When it comes to being grateful it's so much easier when it is part of our DNA, but if it isn't part of your nature don't lose faith, for with a bit mindfulness it will be. We cannot be in control of our past experience but we can be an influence on what we aspire to be and experience in our future and that starts today. Gratitude is a constant opportunity for us to show up in life. The potential energy awaiting us in every moment of gratitude, whether it be in embracing gratitude from another person or expressing gratitude ourselves, is an epic gift.

1. For the highest potential to flow, it is important to both be able to gift gratitude;
2. and most importantly, to receive it.

The significance of this is paramount to maintaining a high vibration in our lives. It's a circular exchange that we need not think about too much but it is beneficial to be aware of the power of this simplistic interaction so that we don't become blocks. Allow gratitude to flow in your life to and from others and the results will be visible in no time. Embrace an attitude of gratitude every day!

Begin and end every day with gratitude.

HOW GRATITUDE CAN SERVE YOU

Gratitude is a choice, a smart choice. You could spend all of your time having battles with people, living at a low vibration and fighting your way through life, or you can choose to come from a higher stance and inject gratitude into everything you do. Gratitude is more than a choice. It's a feeling, it's an essence. It becomes part of you.

Make the choice to embrace gratitude. If it's a struggle for you initially, create it as a habit. Do a 21-day habit challenge where you practise gratitude mindfully for 21 days, and it then becomes a subconscious habit. It becomes easier and second nature for you. But how gratitude can serve you is when you allow it to become part of you, and then you make choices through that. And the reason that it serves you is because:

1. It comes from a really good energetic manifestation space.
2. You'll always get the best-case scenario out of anything that you apply it to, whether that is an interaction, an intention or a goal, and whether it is for yourself or others.

When you embrace gratitude, you are at peace with the world, you are in a state of flow. You end up in a very high vibration because not only is gratitude one of the highest virtues, it's also productive and will serve you well. So if you're smart, you will embrace gratitude in your life because it will serve you, it will get you results.

When you are grateful with an open heart and there is love behind it, people will feel that energy and that action will cause a positive reaction in most cases. Sometimes it will conjure up things within others that they don't like about themselves and that can lead to a negative reaction, but they're not your people so don't give them any energy. Save your gratitude for those people who react beautifully to it.

And that's how gratitude serves you. It serves you well, as in, you show up, you put the energy into it because it does require energy. If you put the energy into it, you will get the results in all aspects of your life. Here is an example that comes to mind, and you can check this out in the gratitude stories at the end of this book.

I had a conversation about gratitude with Intuitive Life and Business Coach Joanna Hunter. Joanna talks about how people like to feel appreciated, and when you have appreciation for each other, then the to-ing and fro-ing between you, the interactions between you come from a more genuine place, a place of love. Whereas whenever someone doesn't feel appreciated, they can become resentful. I know that when I apply gratitude to any interaction with anybody I connect with, I always get a better response no matter what.

I always choose gratitude but not overly in-your-face, swamping-you gratitude, just honest down to Earth goodness. It's become second nature. Now gratitude beams from me because I embrace it. And I love it when someone feels gratitude for me, I love the reaction. Even if I don't get the usual reaction, I love to give gratitude because when it lands with someone, it shifts something within them.

Maybe they're not used to receiving that type of energy sent their way but you've made a change. You've ignited something and even if it's an initial rejection, it's still there. They'll carry it forward with them. And that's pretty special.

Gratitude is a gift to the world and a gift to yourself as it will always serve you. People will remember you as the person who gifted that to them because people always remember how you made them feel rather than the details of your interaction. Gratitude serves us well in both business and personal forums.

It serves me well as a mother. Maybe I'm frustrated because I've got some work on and I need a bit of space to do it but my kids are looking for my energy. There's no point doing battle with that. I may as well stop, close the computer and give them some energy, let them know how grateful I am for them and pour my love into them.

It's a mindfulness, a choice. I could sit and try to get the work done, but I would never get anything worthwhile done in that energy and I'm always mindful of that. When I choose to close the computer and be grateful and show gratitude to my children, that's when I get the best out of them. They are pure, pure form, and they are there to test the boundaries. They are there for us to see the best and the worst in ourselves. That's what children do because they are growing. They're curious. They are true energy and sometimes without a filter. Most of us have been conditioned so much by the time we reach adulthood that we do need to reconnect with our inner child. We also need to embrace the essence of gratitude with our children. By me showing it to my children, they can show it back to me.

    Make the right decision. Choose gratitude and let it serve you.

Use gratitude to hack into higher vibrational energy.

GRATITUDE AND MONEY

When you're grateful for the money you have, you will automatically without conscious effort be creating an energetic flow that comes back to you because with every action there's always a reaction. It's all part of the universal laws. Whether or not you know it and are working consciously with those laws, if you have a positive grateful thought about the money you already have in your life, then you will experience more money coming back in.

That's how it goes. There's no point overthinking it. The money that comes into your life as a result of that positive energy is beautiful money. More good people in the world need to think good things about money, because when good people have money, good things happen.

It's important to remember that. When you're grateful for what you have and open to receiving, can you imagine what can happen? Imagine what conscious gratitude around money would help to bring about in your life. We've talked about gratitude and the law of attraction. If you are thinking about the money you want to have in the future, you don't think about the lack of it in the present.

You need to be fully in the gratitude and the energy of what it would be like to have more money in your life. Sit in that energy, in a present mindful moment, really consciously owning and thinking about what your life would be like. What would the essence of your life be like if you had the money you wanted? It needs to be believable for you.

One of my Seven Life Principles is belief. You need to believe it is possible for you to have all the money you want in your life. If you're just dreaming while believing it's impossible, then it will never be possible. If you think it's beyond you, it will always be beyond you. It's important to sit in the energy of what you want so that it's completely believable for you to experience it, because the only limitations on what you can achieve are those you put on yourself. Quite often that is due to limiting beliefs or past experiences.

So do it slowly. Raise your gratitude for money and be grateful for the money you have now, but consciously be grateful for the money you want to have in your future by feeling what it would be like to already have it. My heart flutters with absolute excitement when I think of what I have, what I'm going to have in my future. Just remember, money doesn't bring happiness, but money does bring opportunities for happiness to happen.

It's not bad to have nice things. It's actually beautiful to be opulent, and it's so much more fulfilling and rewarding. When the money comes from a good source, you've earned it or you've manifested it in a beautiful way. So why not you? If it's not you, it'll be somebody else. Money is a positive in your life if you allow it to be by being grateful for it.

We all know how to be grateful. But do you know how to be consciously grateful? This book will show you how.

Embrace it. Enjoy it. It's there for all to have should we choose it.

Being grateful for litlle things emits the same energy as something big.

GRATITUDE OR RESENTMENT?

I'm generally a grateful person, but I am also human and sometimes I feel resentment. Quite often resentment is the initial emotion when we feel an injustice has been done to us, someone isn't meeting our expectations or we are disappointed in some way. Resentment can be generated by different things for different people. I like to hang out in positivity so I don't experience resentment very often but when I do, it's hard for me to shift it because I have to process why I am feeling resentment.

Is it me or is it them? It's always both parties, but I may be more aware of it than the other person, which could be due to us not having had the necessary conversation. Resentment often comes from a place where a conversation needs to be had. A conversation often clears the air and can help someone realise something that they weren't seeing.

When I start to feel resentment, I try to understand why this emotion is being conjured up within me. If I can see what's behind my response and can understand the dynamic there, then it's up to me whether I choose to learn and grow from it.

Generally feeling resentful offers an opportunity for deepening understanding, because resentment is a conflict within yourself. There are emotions tied to a conflict within your heart and mind. That's why resentment holds hard and your mind will create stories around it, because there are always stories. The wonderful Adriana Peters talks about the science of story, and the way we generate and create all different stories around an experience, whereas our perspective will be different than somebody else's perspective. Whether it's in a relationship, in a work situation or with your children, there are all sorts of dynamics that come into play.

I want to offer you an alternative to shift your perspective on resentment, rather than trying to avoid it. Create the understanding. Why am I feeling resentful? And is this an opportunity to discover something about myself and how I interact with others and that I can in turn be grateful for? Be grateful for the learning, because when you have the inner conflict and have the conversation around it and do the learning well, you reach a higher plane.

And when you reach a higher plane, something shifts around you energetically. Whenever resentment comes, you get out of it quicker and so it's really something to be grateful for. Not that we warrant bad behaviour, but there's a kind of freedom in forgiving yourself and someone else. Deeper than the forgiveness is the understanding.

There's a lot to be grateful for around that because of the learning that can happen in this space. So take a moment and think, *why am I resentful?* Go there within yourself. Believe me, when you live at a higher vibration, resentment doesn't come around often or stay long but when it does, you will see that it's below the high vibration. Therefore, it's something we can use as a leveraging tool for change within ourselves and within others if they choose it as well.

If you want something in the future be grateful for it now.

GRATITUDE AND KINDNESS

Kindness is important to discuss around the subject of gratitude because they are both of the same essence. When kindness walks hand in hand with gratitude, beautiful things happen. A little quote that came into my arena recently about kindness is that kindness is someone who brings warmth and value to somebody with no expectation in return. That's why gratitude walks so beautifully with kindness, because the to-ing and fro-ing of giving and receiving without any expectation is something beautiful.

I love giving. I receive a lot in giving energetically, but a lot of people don't understand or see that depth in giving.

Some people give to receive. That's not me. I don't give with any expectation, because whenever somebody does choose to react it doesn't always happen in that moment. Sometimes it's not an instant reaction.

Some people like to simply tick the box of giving. But if you think about the kindness of giving from an energetic, universal laws perspective, Karma refers to what you give out coming back to you. It does though it either comes back to you from the person you give it to or goes to another. We shouldn't try to control that with expectation because time and circumstance align and that's where the magic happens.

Just because we choose to give something to someone, it may not be the right time for them to give to us. They may not be in a good place. They may need kindness shone down upon them, and they will carry it in their hearts, and they will find a way to repay you. And that is beautiful. If you are a person who expresses kindness, don't stop because someone doesn't understand the universal laws and the flow around it. Don't stop the flow. We need that energetic flow in our world.

If you are someone who blocks kindness, if kindness makes you feel uncomfortable, maybe think about it a different way. You could choose gratitude rather than repelling the kindness because gratitude allows it to free flow onto a very high energetic vibration which will serve you and also the person who's being kind. Why would you not choose that more than another negative way?

One time I was in a shop and didn't grab my groceries and go. I had a high vibe happening that day, and as I walked down one of the aisles there was a woman stacking shelves. I said, 'Hello, how are you going today?' It caught her off guard and she smiled back and said, 'I am fine. Thank you for asking.' It lifted her spirits.

I expected nothing in return and it wouldn't have mattered if she didn't smile back. I was just going to infuse that kindness into her day because I got a sense that she needed it. We don't need validation to be kind. We just need to be kind.

I have the pleasure of working alongside the amazing, beautiful Duchess of York. She's the Kindness Ambassador, and is one of the kindest people I know. She's very mindful of others.

We need to open ourselves up and allow our children to understand the value in kindness and all the virtues. We need to bring it into the schools. We need to understand the value of kindness at a younger age so it becomes second nature to us. Let's do that. Let's embrace kindness. It's not giving yourself to somebody, it's pouring that energy into another. And my goodness, it pours back into you.

Did you know we can talk about the kindness quotient in the same way as there is an intelligence quotient or IQ? Have you ever thought about what your kindness quotient might be? I invite you to use the link below to find out your KQ. How kind are you? Be honest with the questions. And I'd love for you to come to the Life Magic with KP Weaver FB group and share your Kindness Quotient.

There is always something to be grateful for, even on the darkest day there will be light.

THE SCIENCE OF GRATITUDE

There is a great deal of research around the science of gratitude and how beneficial it is for us, and I'll share links at the back of this book. I want to keep it basic here so feel free to do your own research. I'm sharing research that resonates with my heart because what resonates with my heart often resonates with my readers' hearts.

I don't like to get things too complicated so let's focus on the wonderful things that gratitude brings into our lives and the science behind it. Did you know that gratitude increases happiness by 25%? Many of us strive for happiness every day so if you want to be happier, start bringing gratitude into your life.

Did you know that gratitude improves your health? Studies show that a grateful mind is linked to healthier blood pressure and heart rate, as well as a stronger immune system and less aches and pains. It's because feeling gratitude and having a happier heart reduces our stress levels and that has a wonderful impact on our health.

People who express gratitude sleep better. This positive trait leads to better quality and longer sleep. When you look at the research, there are very good reasons to practise gratitude from a health point of view — decreased blood pressure, especially for those with hypertension, increased energy levels, reduced stress and physical symptoms, improved sleep quality and a longer life expectancy.

In business, you achieve goals faster, you're more productive, you have fewer sick days, you're better focused, you retain customers, and are more prosperous. From a self-learning perspective, you're more optimistic about yourself. Feeling gratitude benefits your brain and improves your memory, making learning easier. It has a positive effect on relationships, leading to deeper, more thoughtful connections and kinder interactions with others. When you're grateful, all of those things come into play.

Research shows gratitude has a positive effect on all those areas of your life — your health, your business and career, your finances, self-learning and your relationships. They all come together and flow and blend together. You can focus on one aspect but gratitude covers them all. It enhances them all. Why would you not choose to do that? I don't understand why anyone would choose differently.

Researchers always find that people who embrace and express gratitude are happier, healthier and more energetic.

So if you want to stay young at heart, be grateful. The more a person is inclined towards gratitude the less likely they are to be stressed, lonely, depressed, anxious or suicidal.

So how do you show gratitude? You can give out compliments, make lists of things you are grateful for, volunteer in your community. Do small, random acts of kindness, and smile. It does not have to be complicated, but it does take a bit of rhythm and routine to share gratitude in your life.

These three small acts when practised daily will have a big impact: handwritten notes, small acts of kindness and daily gratitude check-ins.

Smile in gratitude and your heart will open.

PASSING THE BATON

There are many times in my life when I chose gratitude instead of a negative reaction or thought. Gratitude is a productive action in your mind and in your heart. When you choose gratitude and express gratitude in your mind, in your heart, if you write it, if you action it, it makes things happen in your life and around you. As I write this, I feel gratitude because I can make choices. I feel gratitude that I have the ability to love, and to feel that love is something to truly be grateful for, and we all have the ability to do that.

We all have the ability to stop for a moment, pause and just get into that energy. But it does take that bit of mindfulness to say to ourselves, 'Okay, let's not do busy for a moment. Let's stop and have the mindful moment to be grateful, because I want more for myself. I want to get into the habit of the rhythm of living at a higher vibration, of having more for myself and my family, of having more in my life. I want more in my future. So right now, I'm going to be grateful for what I have and in my future I will have more.'

It's as simple as that. But the practice of gratitude has to be done with an open heart for the benefits to really filter through. We need to feel it. We need to feel emotion in it. We need to feel as much as we can to really get the potential out of each gratitude moment.

We can say 'I am grateful for this and for that' but if you don't have the feeling, the emotion and the energy in your gratitude, you're never going to get the results. Usually, people who are sceptical about gratitude have shown gratitude and not seen any results. They either expected the results immediately, which doesn't always happen, or they expected them to come in a particular way.

There is always an impact. If you are mindful and your mind is open and you're aware of what's around you, you will see the results instantly, but they're never going to be what you expected because they show up in different ways. They're not conventional. But when you are mindful and aware and you have your peripheral vision on, you'll have an observation. You will feel something more beautiful around you and your energy. You start attracting the right things and the right people into your circle and you'll be gifted the opportunity to let go of that and those that don't serve you. Be grateful for that because some people are in our life for a season, and some are in our life for a lifetime. We're supposed to learn what we need to learn from them and then move on.

Be grateful for the opportunity to declutter and be grateful to let go of all that doesn't serve you. Don't hold on to it because it will go to someone who needs it for their next stage, for their manifestations. We need to let go so that somebody else can pick up the baton and run with it and do their part of the relay of life.

Wouldn't it be beautiful if we all thought that way? If we all thought of the person coming behind us, and were grateful for them to come and take the baton so that we could then be free to run and grab the next baton that's there for us. Think of life as that relay, that full circle. We run, run, rest. We pause for a moment to recalibrate, reenergise, and then once we have our cups full, we move on to the next race. Life is about that. We bring our new learning from the previous race to the next race because we always learn something about ourselves and others on that journey.

I'm grateful that I'm aware of the cycles of life, and I'm grateful that I'm able to share my awareness with you so that you too can become aware of them. It's important to understand how our life works and how we choose to go in these cycles. We can't just keep going around in circles in the one cycle; we need to stop, pause, detach from that cycle and move on to the next one. It's like moving on to another chapter. You can't keep writing the same chapter.

Our life needs to move on as we create new experiences. It's important to be grateful for our life cycles and the awareness of them; to enjoy each cycle, each new beginning, each ending, each journey, each destination, each baton handed to us.

We need to be grateful for it all, every lesson that is learned. Let's enjoy it all. Let's move forward in love and gratitude.

I am happy because I choose gratitude every day.

GRATITUDE, YOUR CHOICE

You may have heard the saying, 'You can lead a horse to water, but you can't make it drink.' The same goes for the power of gratitude. I can share all the insights in the world in this book but if you don't act on them, they're worth nothing. You will not see results.

That saying always reminds me of when I was around 18 years old. A group of us arranged to go riding and I told the people who managed the horses that I could ride. Yet I had never been on a horse in my life and knew nothing of how to manage one. The horse I was on took off at a gallop and I was so afraid because I did not know how to stop it. I thought I was going to be seriously injured, if not die because it galloped on and on. I was in absolute despair. It galloped and galloped until it got to the water's edge, where it stopped for a drink. It must have been really thirsty and I nerdiered over its head.

This horse wanted the water so much and it was being held back. It was only when it got the freedom, albeit with me on its back, that it galloped to water. So if you're thirsty for gratitude, if you're thirsty for what gratitude can do in your life, gallop to that water's edge and start to action it in your life.

When you reap the rewards of the gratitude and are aware of the results you are getting because you are actioning it, it's the most magnificent thing to experience. It's all well and good to say, 'I am grateful' but that's not action. Those are words. Yes, words are powerful, but words with meaning, with feeling, with purpose are more powerful.

It's your choice and nobody can make it for you. Nobody can do it for you. You can say the words, but if you don't mean them, it's not going to have any effect in your life.

Choosing gratitude is the simplest way to change your life in a short time. It's immediate.

I always choose gratitude. I'm so grateful for the love of my children. I'm so grateful for the opportunities that come my way. I'm so grateful for the beautiful home I'm in. I'm so grateful for my relationships. I'm so grateful for my family.

I'm so grateful that I'm happy and I've chosen to prioritise joy. I'm grateful for lots of things. I could list 100 things right now that I'm grateful for because there's always something to be grateful for even on your darkest day.

Choose gratitude because there's always a glimmer of hope. If you are alive, if you're breathing, that is something to be grateful for.

There's always someone worse off than us. It's about owning our own lives and doing amazing things should we choose to enjoy gratitude.

Being grateful helps others receive you.

GRATITUDE AND YOUR VISION.

I wanted to bring this chapter into the gratitude book because I have had a lot of success with visualisation. No, I don't do it a lot. I don't do it every day like some people do. I consciously do it when I'm called to.

One thing I've observed is that when I am in a space of gratitude before I visualise, it's so much more powerful, it manifests things so much more quickly and it helps clarify the visualisation. Visualising is individual for everyone, but for me it's where I go into a kind of day dream, and there are no limitations, there's no judgement, there's only dreams and love, gratitude and happiness and joy. I allow my perfect scenario to play out in front of me in my visualisations.

I just embrace and feel the essence of that. And I think because I do it in gratitude, the manifesting happens. As self-help author Bob Proctor said, if you can see it in your mind, you can have it in your hand. A lot of people don't realise that when you visualise something it's like setting an intention, and when you prefix it with gratitude, it is so much more powerful.

So if you do visualisation, do it in the essence of gratitude. If you're consciously visualising, do your gratitude beforehand. An example of this is when I visualised myself in my dream house at the beach. I didn't have a visual of the house, but I did have the essence of it, as in I wanted six bedrooms, I wanted to be at the beach, and I used to just dream about it.

It's not that I didn't believe it was possible, I did, but I never thought it was the right time for it. But that's not up to me to judge. And it turned out the right time was sooner than I anticipated and I'm here now. In what I call a bizarre moment of fate the most magical place at the perfect scenario was handed to us and it's been perfect. One thing with visualising and incorporating gratitude, you need to also have faith that when time and circumstance align, the magic will happen. No sooner, no later, just right in the perfect moment.

Now, you may push and you may try to control the journey but it will not happen as perfectly as it will when it's time for it, so embrace that. Allow it to happen and watch the magic in motion.

My tips for prefixing visualisations with gratitude are to spend some time listing off what you are grateful for that day or that week and also to be grateful for the things you're about to see and feel and do in your visualisation. When it comes to practising visualisation, go to a place where you like to be. I have a writing desk that overlooks the sea. I love it and it's a perfect place for me to go into the essence of a visualisation. I've often visualised really well on the back patio of our old house and always very much in gratitude, and also in love.

Oh, my goodness, I love my life and it loves me back. When you visualise in that kind of energy, things happen so much faster so try to get into a space of gratitude. You don't have to stay in a visualisation for any set time. Do what works for you and take action when opportunities aligned with that visualisation present themselves in the world. For me, that usually happens fast, sometimes in a few hours or the next day though it could be a week or two weeks. Just have faith but be ready to take action when needed.

Gratitude is one of the most beautiful virtues to embrace.

IF YOU WANT IT, BE GRATEFUL FOR IT NOW

This way of thinking defies everything we have been programmed to believe so you will need to have some faith in the process for it to reach its highest capacity. I can assure you that when you use this correctly it will change your life for the better.

Being grateful for what we have now, both the big and the small things, will bring more of that goodness into our lives and that is wonderful. But what if you could next level the immediate impact in your life to manifest the future of your dreams?

You can! You can do it by being grateful for what you want in the future whilst making yourself subconsciously believe that you have it now. In this way you can trick your mind and subsequently your energy to bring in your heart's desire. I have used this on many occasions and it works so I don't question it, I embrace it.

On many occasions I have observed people building some momentum only to undo the magic in motion by overthinking and talking themselves out of it. WHY?

Live, love and be grateful!

GRATEFUL PARENTING

Our children are our biggest challenges and our biggest accomplishments. There's no one size fits all when it comes to any child. I'm a mother of six and every one of my children has required a different version of me to parent them.

They come out of the same person and yet they're so different, they don't even look the same. So how do we show gratitude as a parent? Being a parent is one of the most challenging things that you will ever experience in your lifetime and yet one of the most rewarding. I endorse grateful parenting because it always helps me to see the good in any scenario.

When kids play up, I try to see it from a different perspective. Sometimes they need a bit of the tough loving where we say, 'no, that is not okay'. When we're trying to guide our children so that they can be strong enough to make their own decisions rather than control them, that's when wonderful things happen. Every night I'm grateful for each one of my children and I'm grateful for their health. I always say that I'm grateful for their health because when I'm grateful for their health, they're healthy.

My kids rarely get sick and if they are, I just give them so much love. One of my girls has been diagnosed with type one diabetes and that was a big shock to our family. It doesn't mean there's anything wrong, she just has this to deal with and she's going to be fine.

But I'm so grateful she's alive. I'm so grateful that she's making progress. She just has to pause for a moment in life and find her way again and that's okay. We're here to support her. Whenever you're a grateful parent, it gives you the energy that you need to parent.

If you are feeling the stress of being a parent, if you are feeling very heavy and burdened, then you won't have the energy required to be the parent you want to be. It's as simple as that. So that's when it's time to hold up your hand and say I need a break. I certainly do from time to time. We all need a break every now and again.

Even when we try to take the time to be our best version of ourselves, sometimes we're tired or scenarios happen and we end up turning into the parent we don't want to be. And that is life. And that is okay.

You know, all is wonderful.

*Happiness can easily be found
in a grateful heart.*

GRATEFUL RELATIONSHIPS

Be grateful for your relationships. Whether it's your intimate relationship with a partner, your children or with friends, be really grateful for the bonds. Seek out the good in those relationships, focus on that and be grateful for it. Relinquishing expectation can help you to feel gratitude for others.

That's something I've always been good at but you do need to watch out for toxic people who are there to take advantage of that. It's interesting to observe relationships in action. You can have positive and negative thoughts around a relationship and that will have an impact on the relationship. Focus on the relationship negatively and you will have a negative experience of it. Focus on it positively and you will have a more positive experience of it.

I know from experience that no matter how strong your mind is, when your heart is involved, it can be tough or so wonderful. It's about getting that balance right and knowing who energises you and who's worth the effort. You need to choose that for you. No metaphysical book or anybody else can do that for you. That is your responsibility.

You choose who you want to have around you, who you want to energise you, or if you do choose someone that maybe hangs out in the negative, just pray that you rub off on them a little bit. But if they're toxic, no matter how much positive energy you pump into that person, they are never going to fill you up, they're never going to energise you. It is only ever going to be a one-way scenario and they're going to be an energy vampire. They're going to take the energy from you and they're not going to share it around. That's not how the universe works so it's important for us to have active relationships with people.

We can be connected to someone in our family, or to someone who isn't the best person in the world, but that doesn't mean we are actively in a relationship with them. We might only see them at a birthday or a wedding or casually. But if you are actively connecting and having a relationship with someone, whether it is intimate, or with your children, your family or in a friendship, if it's an active relationship that is toxic it will take away from you. If it's an active relationship that involves two-way giving, there's love in it, and it's energising. So it's up to you.

But be grateful for all relationships, because through their intricacies they all help us to grow. Some toughen us up, some soften us down. What is important is to always keep the love in your heart unshielded, because nothing should ever make you shield your heart. The love always needs to be active, always needs to be open, always needs to be pouring into someone or something.

And when you're being grateful for the relationships you have, focus on those that deserve your love. Pour into them and allow them to pour into you and wait to see the difference in your life.

Disappointment dissolves in a cup filled with gratitude.

HAPPY DANCE WITH GRATITUDE FOR NEXT LEVEL IMPACT

Goodness me. When something happens that you've been waiting or hoping for, something on your bucket list, stop and smell the roses because if you don't, you're missing out on a happy dance moment. If you don't action an inspired thought in the moment of it, it goes and in the same way, if you don't happy dance in a happy dance moment, it passes. So don't let it pass. Grab it, celebrate it.

Let the world know. Let that ball of energy come from deep

within you, from every atom in your body. Let it beam from you, that energetic pulsation that emits from your body. It is an amazing magnet that attracts more of it to you. I have had these moments often. One of the biggest years of happy dance moments for me was 2020 yet the rest of the world was going through a pandemic. I didn't feel guilt because I thought, well, our world needs more people having happy dance moments so we can start to fix and heal it. The world was gripped by the energy that surrounds fear around health. The pandemic was real, people were dying and it was horrendous and so many people were affected by it.

And yet here I was in my little bubble in Perth, Western Australia, where we had closed borders and less exposure to the pandemic. I felt so much empathy for people elsewhere, but I knew the world needed us to embrace what was happening. For me on a personal level it was important to be able to emit happy dance moments, to show that life was still happening, to say, 'Don't get entrenched in the news.'

From a metaphysics perspective, the mind comes before the body and your body reacts to what your mind is thinking. The mind is powerful and when it is overwhelmed with unhealthy thoughts, guess what? You become unhealthy. And when you become unhealthy, overwhelmed, tired or rundown, living at a low vibration, it hits you like a rocket.

What the world needs is for us to have our happy dance moments with deep gratitude for what's happening and what we are making happen in the world. We do that by celebrating the wins, sharing those wins with people so that they can get the vibe and go, 'Wow, world, things are still happening for people. There's hope, there's a glimmer.' I'm not sharing to rub it in your face. I'm sharing so that you can see there are still good things happening for good people.

So happy dance with gratitude for next level impact, because you have to, because the world needs you to, because your community needs you to, because your family needs you to, because you need you to, too.

That energy is healing energy. That energy is manifesting energy. That energy makes a difference. And it is not selfish. It is fruitful, it is energising and it is very important.

Appreciating what others do helps
relationships blossom.

GRATITUDE IN BUSINESS

I have always loved the concept of being grateful in business. Gratitude is deemed to be something for our personal not professional life, but I know from experience that when you bring gratitude into the workplace it has great results.

If you are in business or are planning to launch a business venture, incorporate gratitude in all the connections you make. It lets people know that you acknowledge and appreciate what they have done for you.

It's so important that we take time to be grateful in our business, and it needs to become second nature. Not that we need to bombard people with it, but just taking a moment to send a gift, or write an email that isn't rushed but written with more connection makes a difference. Build a rapport with the people you do business with in an authentic, genuine way.

You're not just looking for the money. You are wanting to work with the person and you want to get to know them. Everybody's different. I'm in publishing and one of the things I love about my business is getting to know my authors. There's a lot of work in publishing and it can be stressful at times for some people because of the journey they're on. I always make time to go on the journey with them and it's always amazing.

Taking a moment to be grateful and show gratitude in our actions as well as our words makes people feel valued when you are doing business with them. They're not just a number. That's the focus in my business because I genuinely love connecting with the people whose journey I'm sharing. There will always be some people who are your people and some people who aren't, and that's okay. But when you do go on the journey with someone, it makes good business sense to keep that integrity with you, to be grateful and to really connect.

I get called into business arenas now to speak on the Power of Knowing, which is one of my seven life principles. When you know how to *know*, you can make decisions with unwavering faith that where you're going is the right direction. It saves you time, energy and mistakes. It's the same with gratitude. You can use gratitude as a tool to bring on a new client and if they push it away or react to it badly, then they are not your client. You do not want to take them on board.

Perhaps they're simply not used to it yet. But if someone has a real issue with you being grateful, then they're going to have an issue with a lot of other things on the journey with your service so it'll end up costing you energetically and probably financially by the end of your contract with them. I always start with gratitude and see how they react to it, and then I use it as a kind of gauging tool as to whether they are my ideal client or not. My ideal clients are able to appreciate gratitude because they understand the value in it, they understand I'm going to do my best for them and they are grateful in return, which means I want to do more for them.

That's the way the universe works and anyone who's resistant to that is resistant to the process of evolution, of things happening, so there are going to be a lot more blocks. Gratitude can be a really good gauging tool when bringing on clients. Try it!

Gratitude is love.

BEING GRATEFUL WHEN YOU DON'T FEEL IT

Being grateful even for the hard lessons is a tough one, it really is.

The hard lessons weigh heavy on our hearts. They force us to go inward. They're uncomfortable. They bring us out of ourselves because what we thought to be is not the case. That's a tough lesson to learn, especially if you've invested a lot of emotional energy in making something happen.

So how do we change our perspective from shame, anger, pain, sadness, all of those darker emotions? How do we salvage what we can, and have a positive reaction to these tough times? Gratitude is the way out. In *The Visitor* I used a quote at the beginning that I did not know at the time would be the essence of that book.

'From every negative situation, there is the potential for a positive outcome.'

If you are not aligned with your intentions and goals, with your highest potential, the universe will halt you in your tracks every now and again to make you stop and re-evaluate, reassess and get some clarity. Sometimes it can be a big shock to the system. Your nervous system physically gets shocked, and you have to pause and process what's happened. It's not a time for action.

Please note that. It's not a time for action. But no matter how dark any day is, there's always something to be grateful for.

So find it. Let it shine through. Let it carry you through, and let something amazing come from that.

What are you grateful for today?

GRATITUDE AFFIRMATIONS

It pays huge dividends to choose gratitude. The energy in your atoms will be happier and your results will speak for themselves!

Gratitude helps you instantly rewire old thinking patterns. It can be easily embraced with a simple shift in perspective.

On the next page I have compiled 20 common gratitudes. I would love for you to add 10 more.

1. I am grateful for the life I have.
2. I am grateful that I have choices.
3. I am grateful to be able to give and receive unconditional love.
4. I am grateful for self-love.
5. I am grateful for my friends.
6. I am grateful for all the opportunities that come my way.
7. I am grateful for inspired thoughts and actions.
8. I am grateful for my personal freedom.
9. I am grateful that I can make a difference in this world.
10. I am grateful for my family.
11. I am grateful for my occupation.
12. I am grateful for laughter.
13. I am grateful for my interests.
14. I am grateful for my home.
15. I am grateful for the food I eat.
16. I am grateful for my daily walk.
17. I am grateful that I am me.
18. I am grateful for time.
19. I am grateful when someone takes a moment to connect.
20. I am grateful for beautiful places and experiences.

Add 10 things that you can be grateful for in your life:

1.

2.

3.

4.

5.

6.

7.

8.

9.

10.

Gratitude helps you see the unseen.

LOVE-FUELLED GRATITUDE

One thing I've noticed that sets me and other super manifestors out from the pack is that we embrace love. There is an unlimited supply of love within us all; in fact the more we use love, the more love grows!

Please read this line below until it is ingrained inside you.

When you are grateful with all your heart it is a super fuel!

I know this because I have not only observed it, I have actioned it on many occasions. Not everyone has the ability to open their heart freely. Kids do it but as we become adults, we become distrustful and damaged because of past experiences.

Being grateful with all of your heart becomes a super fuel and it means that you work as one with the universe because the universe *is* love. When we begin to trust and have faith that it works solely for us, and that the energy created through love teamed with the energy of gratitude because gratitude is love, it is a super fuel for success. It will deliver whatever you channel the energy on, so be sure to remain mindful of your intentions around that.

I'm going to share with you a secret hack here, one that super manifestors understand implicitly. Learn to pour love and gratitude into what you want but don't already have and it will come to you. Sit in the essence of feeling that you have it right now for a few minutes a day, then watch and wait as it finds its way to you. You will know when you need to action the steps but my goodness, wait till you see how fast it comes your way when you pair love and gratitude together and trust in the process.

The world is your oyster, there is nothing you cannot achieve. Keep it simple. Too often we make it complicated. You need to feel unconditional love and have total faith in your ability to manifest. Be grateful for what it feels like to have the thing that you want in your future. Sit in the essence of what that would be like and the best way to do that is in visualisation. Close your eyes and just sit with it, because if we can create it in our mind, we can create it in our reality.

You need to know what you want and be open to feeling what it is like to receive it. Pump loving energy and gratitude into that moment because not only is it in your head it's in your heart. Once you bring it through your head and heart it starts to vibrate through your body, and it becomes real in the senses before you even have it in your hands or experience it in reality. It actually becomes real in that moment of manifestation. It is the most powerful process in the whole of existence and when you have learned the power of love-fuelled gratitude you will never manifest any other way.

Count your blessings, not your heartaches.

IRISH PROVERB.

THE GRATITUDE JOYRIDE

When we are joyful, we raise our vibration and that's contagious. Others can benefit from our energy. It energises them as well, so it has a ripple effect.

I remember a time when I chose joy. I used to write for a magazine called *Universal Mind*. I think I had four children at the time and may have been pregnant with my fifth. However, I went to visit the magazine owner, who didn't live far from me. She invited me over and it was very serendipitous how she started finding my writings and using them in her magazines.

But that's another story. What I wanted to share with you was that she said she wanted to read for me. I'm always open to that so she did a reading using numerology and said, 'Where you are on your life path, you're about to go into a joyride setting. And when that happens, it's just going to be like you're riding the waves like a dolphin.'

'Wow,' I said. 'Cool.'

'No,' she said. 'You don't understand how big it's going to get, but just keep riding the waves, having the fun, enjoying the love of your children because that's what will energise you. And just do it your way. Don't worry about anybody else. Just keep doing what you love and enjoy, and you'll have so much success. It's as if you're just going to be riding the waves. It's big dolphins. That's what I see.'

I've been doing this now for about ten years so in numerology terms I'm probably back full circle on that cycle, which is interesting. One thing I've observed is that over those past ten years I have been on many joyrides. And when you are energised and success is happening and everything is so free flowing and fun, it's energising, it really and truly is.

It also requires you to be very activated all the time. You don't feel tired because you're running on adrenaline. It's fun. I've been on those kinds of life joyrides for six months at a time.

But one thing I'm always mindful of is to really enjoy the power of the pause. When there's a lull and maybe I've planted another seed of intention, I've done what I can to make that happen and it's a quiet period, I usually distract myself with something else. But it's also important to understand that a big part of the process of manifesting is to embrace that down time so that you can replenish those energy fields within you that will fuel the next part of the cycle. We need to step back and cuddle our kids again just to make sure we have that beautiful blend because otherwise we will run out of the joyride rocket fuel.

Love is one of the biggest super fuels for manifesting. You don't want to burn out when you're on a joyride, you want to enjoy every moment of it so it's important to keep your cup full. Our job is to keep moving forward, keep working towards things that bring us joy, that we see in front of us. Just keep taking that next step. Do not think of the big picture. We know the essence of what we want so it is not our job to think of the big picture because that will overwhelm us. All the things that need to happen to get from here to there will overwhelm you and you will run a mile. You'll feel it as overwhelming struggle and you will bail out.

Before any breakthrough there's always a struggle but when you take it step by step you've walked a mile before you realise it's an important milestone. One of your duties when it comes to manifesting, or going on the journey to receiving or whatever you want to call it, is to keep your cup full, because when the joyride comes, you're going to need that energy. You're going to need that cup full and you're going to need reserves for your family. You will also need reserves for other things that you will not have full focus on, so that will enable you to enjoy the rewards that you reap. You won't feel like you've compromised on your values because you've got this beautiful blend of energy, and anyone who loves you will want to see you happy once you keep the lines of communication open and say, 'This is really important, this is a goal that I've been working really hard towards, we'll all reap the benefits of it.'

When that joyride comes, you know it. You have to allow yourself to embrace it and reap the rewards from it because that is high vibe contagious. Everyone will want a piece of that and you have to maximise on that so you can continue to inspire others. Personal development and peak performance pioneer Jack Canfield says one of mistakes made by the great leaders of the past is that they never empowered others with their wisdoms. They kept them to themselves. And that is one of the big things that's wrong with the world. People are keeping things to themselves and they should be sharing with each other. Sharing is how we grow. There's enough for everybody.

In fact, if we're all raising the vibration of the world, the world is going to be a great place for us all, we're all going to benefit. So embrace the joyride, harness the joy. Keep the cup full and pour into those around you.

Rejoice is all that you have in the now.

BEING THE CHANGE – THE WORLD NEEDS MORE GRATITUDE

Imagine a world led by gratitude. Leaders who embrace what it means to appreciate the efforts of others. I look back on many scenarios in history and see that well intentioned actions were often misread, and had the immediate reaction been one of appreciation rather than retaliation it may have changed the course of history. It's not too late to change our reactions to things on a personal and professional level.

Remember it's a universal law! Every action attracts an

equal reaction so it's important to be mindful of how we react to things, how we act and what our intentions are, but to also be mindful of what's around others. I really feel the essence of that, and to be the change we need to be more grateful and kind to each other in the world. When we react and act through the essence of gratitude and kindness, we will see a significant difference in world interactions and connections.

If someone is well intentioned but what they do is wrongly perceived, the reaction to it is totally misaligned to their intention. It's an emotionally fuelled reaction and that's a recipe for disaster. Consider options and count to five before you react, especially if it's going to be an emotional reaction. You could be responding to a trigger from the past. It's just as important to be mindful of people's intentions around their actions as well as your reactions to them. When we do that, especially in leadership, but even on a day-to-day personal level with our families and the people we meet, it will make a positive difference.

Where parenting is concerned, a child is coming from a different place of knowledge, awareness and wisdom. They haven't experienced a lot of life challenges and they have a lot to learn. When they react with a tantrum or in an unexpected way, our reaction is important because they learn from us. We're the adults and in their eyes, we're supposed to have it all together. They're going to learn from our reactions, not from our words so how we act needs to be aligned with what we say.

Be mindful of that also around your connections with adults and understand that people have different levels of emotional intelligence or could be responding to a trigger from a past life that has nothing to do with you. You may just be a catalyst to reaction for somebody who needs to deal with an issue. We don't have to walk around on eggshells but we do need to be mindfully aware because usually energetically we can pick up on this. Especially if you're an open-hearted person and you're dealing with someone who doesn't embrace open-hearted people.

You can bring out the best and the worst in people. Be mindful and accepting of that and don't take too much on board personally because it's not always personal. Be the change that you want to see in the world. Spread more gratitude and kindness wherever you go and we will all see the difference that makes.

Embrace a habit of gratitude for all the things that have contributed to your advancement.

FIND GRATITUDE IN PROCRASTINATION

I want to alter the widely held perspective of procrastination as a negative, as failing, as not showing up. I'm grateful when I procrastinate. I know it can be inconvenient for others, but it means that something's not ready to go out. And it's not often that I procrastinate.

I'm more of an action-based doer than a procrastinator. But when I procrastinate with my writing, for instance, it's because I haven't been in the energy of it or there's something waiting to be realised or the timing is off. There's always a reason. So I want to shift the perspective on procrastination.

It's not that you're failing, it's not that you're behind schedule, it's that you're actually aligned to a higher, more divine timing and you're allowing that to process.

And when it's time, the energy, the motivation and the focus on everything required to get over the line will come to you and you will do it in lightning speed, with total clarity and it will be gold. I'm not just talking about books. I'm talking about projects, about anything you might procrastinate about, even contacting someone. If someone says, 'Let's catch up for coffee' and cancels, it's not that they're failing you, it's because it's not the right time. They want their energy to be aligned and the connection to be more divine.

When connections happen in divine timing, that's when magic happens. And you want magic to happen in your life and in the lives of those you love so take the time to make sure everything is aligned. If you think someone is procrastinating in future, I invite you to take an alternative perspective. Instead of deciding they're being an asshole or they're failing or that they haven't got their shit together, consider that they may be connected to more divine timing, even if they aren't fully conscious of it.

Thank you, is quite simply enough.

GRATITUDE AND HEALTH

Be mindful of your own health journey. Know what that is for you. Know that miracles do happen. Know that you can heal.

There are many cases of hospitals and doctors making people believe they are incurable, and they lose hope. But when you have hope, when you have faith, belief and knowledge that your mind can help you to heal, having a happy heart and a positive attitude can help you defy all odds. That's a superpower. I want to share with you a little story about my dad. I love my dad. He's an amazing man.

A few years after we moved to Australia, he had two strokes, one after the other, a few months apart. And I never felt the distance so much in my life. But one of the things that surprised and shocked me more than anything was that he was so determined and so forward focused and would not accept anything else but that he was going to get better. Within a year he was on an aeroplane to Australia to see me because I just had another child.

He had a walking stick, but he still came and he never let himself be defeated. A year or two later, he had a CT scan of his brain to check the stroke damage and to our shock, his brain was fully healed. Compare that with my grandfather, who was quite happy to believe what the doctor said. After he had a stroke, he just sat in his chair all day. He'd light a fire and sit there in the kitchen or the living room and that was all I ever knew of my granddad.

It's interesting when I compare the two. There's no way my dad would accept that as his destiny. Some people are happy to accept a diagnosis, have an easier life and not take any risks. Had I not taken a risk and become pregnant again after a miscarriage, I would never have had any more children for fear of losing one. My dad could have given in to the fear of having another stroke and enjoyed less of a life. He's getting older, but he's not in any way held back because of what happened.

When we focus on optimum health, we achieve optimum health. So give your brain the gift of that. Visualise yourself healthy. Should you come down with an ailment, know that it's for a reason. Discover what that is for you. If something keeps coming up, you need to address it. Knowing that is so important.

Be grateful for your health, the health you have now. If you don't have your optimum health now, be grateful for optimum health in your future, because when you do that, you are manifesting a healthier future. And do we not all want that?

Don't just accept that you're getting older. Don't just accept that you're getting sicker. Know that whatever you accept in your mind is what you will experience. So don't just accept it. Defy it.

Aim higher. Know that miracles happen because if you believe in yourself and others believe in you, nothing is impossible. Remember the power that's in your mind and in your heart and in every atom of your being to regenerate, to heal. We are forever healing all the time.

Embrace the healing potential that you have. Activate the healing potential that you have. Supercharge the healing potential that you have in your life. And wait till you see the results.

Be grateful for your health now. In the future you will feel the benefits.

Gratitude is an eternal source of love.

GRATEFUL CREATIVITY

I have been through a few lulls in creativity. Sometimes I'm really energetically buzzing but creatively, the juices don't flow. And by creativity I don't just mean my writing, I'm also talking about the manifesting, that free-flowing energy where things happen.

If you're a business owner or if you're trying to achieve something in your life, it's really important to have that energetic flow. It truly is. But you won't have it 100% of the time, I don't believe anybody does. It depends on the circumstances. When we are embracing those things and allowing them to be in flow, then it's amazing what can happen.

Right now, I am in the most beautiful creative energy. There are books pouring out of me, left, right and centre. I've been creative with projects and business ideas and my authors are loving it. But it's hard to sustain that all of the time and to be authentic because creativity is a gift, it's a flow, it's magic. And to be able to have it is an honour, because it's divine creativity.

It's so special. There are golden nuggets that come through it, there are messages to help other people. All of those golden essence things in life come through creative energy, even your finances. If you want to earn extra money, if you want to manifest money, you need creative energy to do that. That's why it's important to be grateful for creative energy, so that you have more of it. Being able to identify it, embrace it and harness it is so important in life when you have things you want to achieve.

Creative energy flourishes beautifully in simplicity, in that lovely energy of joy and happiness. Creative energy comes when you have had enough sleep, because if your brain is tired, it's not going to flare. A lot of people have had the stuffing knocked out of their creative energy following COVID due to foggy brain and exhaustion. 'Long COVID' has been likened to chronic fatigue and it's hard for creative juices to flow when you're in survival mode.

Creativity flourishes when there's a beautiful balance in your soul of happiness, of curiosity, just the sense of being. That's when creativity flows beautifully. So be grateful for it when you have it, because it is worth its weight in gold. Be grateful for it, identify it and really utilise it. Make room for that magic in your life, and you will reap the rewards.

My top tips for embracing and ensuring that you have the maximum amount of creative energy in your life are:

- Remain high vibrational so that you're connected to the Divine, because creative energy is a divine source.
- Get enough sleep.
- Get up early so that you can tap into the creative source, especially if there are goals you want to achieve in business or in life.
- Understand that you're not going to be creative all the time, and that's okay. Don't fear that lull, but do everything you can to nurture the environment for creativity to flourish.
- Love life and it will love you back.

Never try to control how gratitude repays you.

THE NO-FEAR APPROACH TO GRATITUDE

Fear stops any dream in its tracks so it's really important that we have a no-fear approach to gratitude. When we're filled with gratitude, our hearts are open, we're free-flowing, we are embracing the potential of every moment, we're grateful for what we've received and for what we're going to receive. And we can't have any fear around it so when manifesting we have to have trust in the process.

So set the intention, action the inspired thoughts and opportunities, and have no fear around saying yes. Be grateful before, during and after that process, and have no fear that it's all coming together. It is so important to have no fear attached to it because fear will pull any high vibrational energy right down. Fear is a human instinct that is there to protect us but when we are manifesting and wanting to make dreams come true, that road can be a little unsettling.

There's always a struggle before a breakthrough so when we meet challenges or big opportunities come our way, fear always steps up first to allow us the gift of processing and releasing any inhibitions we have around it. It's important that this comes at the beginning, because there's no point in it coming at the end. When any of my authors start to get inhibitions after they have sent me their book, and fear sets in, I always say, 'Just honour it and acknowledge it, but move through it.'

It's good to have the fear at the beginning of the process because then when your book is being released and put out into the world, you've already dealt with that, you're already a step ahead. Fear is not your enemy. Fear is there to help you process and move through and honour and acknowledge any inhibitions that may come up around an experience.

There are all different scenarios but I like to use the author one as a good example. Authors will be grateful that they've written a book, but when the book is written and they have started to move into the publishing process, then they realise that this book is going to be out in the world. That can bring up feelings of fear but they're thinking too far ahead.

It's important to acknowledge the fear because when you acknowledge it, you're giving it energy and moving past it so that it doesn't take up any more of your energy. You can move forward with faith and courage to make that goal happen. So honour and feel the fear and do what you want to do anyway.

Whenever you are manifesting or whenever anything is happening, be grateful. Gratitude will get you through those moments of fear. Fear does start to peek through but you don't want to suppress it, you don't want to push it down.

You want to honour it and release it and move on from it. *Hi, fear, how are you going? I see you wearing your ugly head. It's all right, it's cool. I'm fine. Here, I've got this.*

And the fear will leave you. *All right. She seems cool. She seems so fierce in the process, we'll trust her.*

My three top tips for having a no-fear approach to manifesting

- Embrace gratitude. Pour positive energy into anything that you're doing and it will help you to stay high vibrational so that you can move past fear.
- Don't suppress the fear. Acknowledge it, move through it and honour it.
- Understand that fear has its place. For many people, fear is part of the process, and understanding and realising that is important, but it doesn't have to be the roadblock that it is. Don't let it pull you down too much.

A grateful heart is a happy heart.

GRATITUDE IN MOTION STORIES

Amanda Gore

"It isn't what you have in your pocket that makes you thankful, but what you have in your heart."
ANONYMOUS

Do we really have any idea of the truly immense nature of our hearts? People think the brain is the most important organ in the body but it's not! The heart is! The heart rules the rest of the body and the Institute of Heart Math has plenty of scientific evidence to prove it. Visit www.heartmath.com. It's a wonderful organisation, teaching people how to appreciate their hearts and how to change their lives by paying attention to the heart and how it really works.

Your heart connects you to everything. The heart is not just a pump that circulates your blood. Your heart is your world! It's the way you connect to God. Your heart is what connects you to others. It, not your brain, is the seat of your innate intelligence. It is your source of intuition, inspiration, love and life. It is an alchemical vessel. Today is your day to spend time with your heart. It breaks; it hurts; it feels; it thinks; it constantly sends messages to the rest of your body orchestrating everything. It is the conductor of a magnificent symphony — you.

Yet in our busy, rushed lives, we rarely stop and take time to tune into our heart's wisdom. Bless your heart today, thank it, listen to it, and through it. It is very wise, but it often speaks very softly — you have to listen carefully. If we regularly take time to listen to our hearts, we can become aware of a feeling or sense of truly knowing whether something is right or not.

Not an emotion, but a deep sense of knowing. I experienced this on the day of my first marriage. I remember walking down that aisle knowing I was doing the wrong thing. I should have listened! Some of you may relate to that! Although it did not last, I am grateful for the lessons that marriage taught me.

It has taken me many years to learn to listen to, and through, my heart and I still have a long way to go! Studying courses called Sacred Service and Spirit Healing has helped me a great deal. Both courses are well worth looking into for those of you interested in truly finding your heart, joy, peace and being of service to the world. Robert and Cheryl Sardello are amazing teachers. Find your heart today. Listen to it. Listen through it. Bless it. Thank it. Keep talking to it, and listening for its guidance in everything you do.

Wear Gratitude Glasses

It is impossible to have a heart full of misery and a heart full of gratitude at the same time. Do you recall the old saying about people who see through rose-coloured glasses, meaning everything they see looks rosy, pink, happy and good? Well, I believe there are people who walk around wearing black glasses. It doesn't matter what is really there — they see black in everything because it's a habit, a pattern; and they unconsciously search for the black in everything.

I would like to introduce the concept of "gratitude glasses" (GG). Put them on every morning and do not take them off till you go to sleep that night. Create a GG habit; a GG pattern! Make a circle between your thumb and index fingers. Put them over your eyes. There! You now have your own gratitude glasses you can take anywhere and use anytime. Teach your children to do this. It's a great gift. What colour are your glasses: Black? Rose? Bored? Angry? What colour gratitude glasses do you wear? You will be amazed at how quickly you feel better. If nothing else, people will smile at you and if you explain why you are wearing the glasses, they will probably ask for a pair.

This is another powerful tip: If you can't sleep, or have trouble sleeping, do the following activity just before you go to bed. Instead of watching some soul-disturbing television program, lie quietly in bed and reflect on your day. Find three things for which you are grateful and focus on them until you fall asleep. It's even better if you write them down. Put your gratitude glasses on if necessary — or maybe you need to put them on your partner. Or you can both put them on. Better still, write them in your gratitude journal, which you can keep beside your bed, and make it part of your nightly ritual. That's the way my mama did it.

When you wake up, immediately find something for which to be grateful. It will transform the nature of your day. Many studies have shown this technique is a powerful antidote to depression and makes us happier.

Examples of seeing your world through gratitude glasses

People who wear Gratitude Glasses
- See traffic delays as happening for a good reason and possibly keeping you safe.
- Make the house they live in a home, no matter how "bad' it is.
- Are grateful they have a family — even a dysfunctional one!

- See themselves as rich no matter how much money they have.
- GGs alter the way you view what happened to you as a child in a reframed way.
- Seeing our food through GG reminds us to bless every meal and to be thankful for it and those who prepared it for us.

Filter what your parents did to you and for you through GG — you may be stronger, more resilient, more compassionate, and more loving as a result of your experiences. People who wear Gratitude Glasses are always reviewing their blessings and giving thanks for them. They help you see the good in everything.

Joanna Hunter

Gratitude for me is like the absolute pinnacle of your spiritual journey. You don't need to learn anything more. If you learn gratitude, you have everything you need, because gratitude for yourself improves yourself. Relationship gratitude for others improves your relationship with others. Gratitude for the money you have increases the money that you have. Gratitude for your environment, your home, the country you live in just increases the satisfaction and contentment in living in those places and things.

For me, gratitude is literally the secret sauce for everything. And one of the things that I discovered really early on in my life coaching practice was that I've had a really unique ability to always see energy. I see it around people. I see it in animals, plants, all the things. I see it in inanimate objects. I used to think everybody could do this and it wasn't until it I was about three or four that I realised, oh, people don't see all the pretty colours that are around everything all the time. So I've had that all my life. And even when I tried to suppress my spiritual gifts, it was the one that just wouldn't go. And so when I got my life coaching clients, I would obviously be coaching them intuitively but I would be looking at their energy fields and seeing. I went through a spate of doing relationships and it wasn't on purpose.

A couple of people were going through a divorce and they came to me and I did such a great job with them they told all their friends. So suddenly it was a massive influx of people having relationship problems. And it didn't matter where these people were in their relationship, whether one partner had cheated, whether they had just simply fallen out of love, whether they were considering leaving their partner, whether they were going through an abusive relationship or whatever was going on in that relationship.

There was the same energy again and again and again so I was asking, what is this energy? I work really closely with my spirit team and they said, 'It's a lack of appreciation.' It was such a huge epiphany moment for me because I realised that the breakdown of any relationship starts with a lack of appreciation. Always. It doesn't matter if one partner cheats on another partner, it started with a lack of appreciation. Or people who just simply drift apart — lack of appreciation. Appreciation is that glue that sticks us together.

I told my husband what I'd observed, that these relationships broke down because of a lack of appreciation and always the women I coached decided they wanted to stay with their partner. We used appreciation to glue them back together, basically, and to heal their relationship. And every time their relationship would heal and become better than ever.

So I said to my husband, 'If a lack of appreciation is what rips the relationship apart, then obviously, appreciation is what connects the relationship together.' We sat down and discussed it for our relationship. And we began really practising gratitude in our relationship, telling each other on a daily basis that we're grateful for each other, grateful for the things that we do for each other. We are grateful to have each other in our lives, these sorts of things. And we've now been married coming up for 25 years.

I would definitely say our relationship is stronger than ever. It's more solid because of gratitude and because of that mindful practice of really appreciating even the small things.

It makes us feel valued within the relationship. Many people fight about the small stuff. It's usually not the big stuff that implodes the relationship. Sometimes it is, but the majority of the time, the small stuff was there to start with.

It's always the little niggles, like leaving the socks on the floor, that start shifting energy. It starts to grate on you and eventually you blow up and then it's the big argument. Whereas when you have appreciation for each other, appreciation builds. When you feel like you're appreciated in a relationship you do more things to keep the appreciation going because you want to be appreciated.

So that's huge for me in our relationship and it's been huge for my clients as well. Many of my clients say, 'You've literally saved my marriage because we appreciate each other so much more now.' And here's the thing — I always call gratitude a bouncy energy. When you give gratitude, it bounces back. So if you say something nice to someone, for instance, 'I really appreciate you in my life, I think you're great', they look for something that they can appreciate about you. It bounces backwards and forwards, and it creates a vibration that moves higher and higher. That's one of the things that I absolutely adore about gratitude. The other reason why I feel it is the only tool anybody needs is that gratitude on the scale of consciousness can calibrate as high as 920. That's a possible thousand, so human beings in physical form can calibrate at the very maximum.

We're in the realms of enlightenment in different stages and degrees of enlightenment from 700 to 1000, so 920 really can bring a human being into a state of enlightenment. What that does is your problems exist on a lower form of consciousness. Your problems exist in lower realms, basically. When you vibrate higher, not only do you live where the solutions are, but you also start to see problems through a different perspective. Problems often become like opportunities at higher functioning consciousness. As your consciousness rises, you start to see a big issue as, 'Oh, actually, this is a really cool opportunity. I could do this or this, and then the problem would be solved'. We see something good comes of it. So gratitude is the easiest, simplest way of really raising your vibration and raising your consciousness because it's something that everyone can do in their present state. Everyone can find something that makes them feel grateful now.

Energy attracts, energy is alive and kicking. And when you put yourself on the vibration frequency of gratitude, it literally gives you more things to be grateful for. When I came to gratitude about 15 years ago, I considered myself quite an upbeat, positive person. I heard about this gratitude practice and I said, 'Okay, well, I'm going to give it a whirl. I've got this.' I was going to write ten things I was grateful for and two hours later, I was sat with tears streaming down my face. I had eight and just could not find two more. I was so frustrated and upset with myself and I thought, 'Oh, my God, this is horrific. I consider myself a positive person. Every single one of those eight, I could have easily written what I was grateful for and then what I disliked.' There wasn't anything that was really in the pure, squeaky clean energy of gratitude. That was a bit of a shocker, an eye opener.

But I decided to go back the next day and try again, but again I got eight. The following day it was nine and the day after that I got ten. Then it got easier as my focus began to switch into gratitude. Now, if somebody was to stop me in the street and say, 'Tell me what you're grateful for', they can't shut me up. There's so much to be grateful for.

I realised that my attitude in life has changed so explicitly, but also very quickly. For a long time, I'd been in hustle mode, trying to build my earlier businesses, which were brick and mortar businesses, working really, really hard, because that's how society told you to do it. I did everything I was told I should and still I felt like the carrot was dangling and I wasn't quite grabbing it.

Within a very short time of engaging gratitude, we got a new house that was three times the size of our old house. I was working 72 hours a week. Soon after really discovering working with gratitude, it went to 18 hours a week and I was earning twice the amount I was earning before things started shifting rapidly.

I realised there is such an easier way. I had spent so much time focusing on everything that I did not want and very little time focusing on what I did like and enjoy and think was good in life. That was the big reverse. Basically, I just reversed the energy. I stopped focusing on what I didn't want and started focusing on what I wanted, and I wanted to feel grateful and I wanted to feel good.

I just kept doing that and it kept building and right now I'm in my office in my well over half a million pound home. Six years ago, I was living on welfare.

It is such a contrast and I know that it was absolutely 100 % the gratitude that got me here. I know that without it, I would not have been able to create what I've been able to create, I wouldn't have the quality of life and the relationships I have. All of my relationships are based on gratitude now.

And I just I love what I do. I absolutely adore my team as well. We have a team of five and they are in such gratitude as well. We get to do this as our job, and they're always so grateful. The number one thing I hear from them is, 'I can't believe I get paid for this, I'm so grateful. I'm so grateful for you. I'm so grateful for your work. I'm so grateful for our clients. I'm so grateful I get this opportunity to do work that I feel is really important in the world.' And that's so beautiful. That takes my breath away.

Our company, Ethos, is based in gratitude as well. It's everywhere in our whole company. That was one of the things that I really wanted to be as an employer, somebody who appreciated the work that my people do. We planned a 100K launch by the beginning of this year and we ended up with three consecutive 100K launches. I treated my whole team to brand new iPads to show them our gratitude and our appreciation for that.

For me, that is better than all the money. I took the whole team to Belfast as well and we had an absolute blast. We went to the Giants' Causeway, we did an escape room. It was so phenomenal. All of it totally expenses paid. I didn't want my team to put their hand in their pockets for the entire weekend. It was beautiful and bonding but at the same time it was for me to show my appreciation of and my gratitude for these people that are really holding me so impeccably. Not only do I get to do the work that I love, I also get to be supported by people that really get it and are adoring it as much as me.

We teach something called 'unity consciousness', which is you in sacred self Union with your truth, which is source, and in fully embodying that truth, therefore becoming magic. So we call our year-long curriculum 'be magic', because what happens to people is that they become more magical when they embody that we have four pillars to be magic.

Pillar One is the self, so it's really learning to love yourself, to be your own cheerleader. In the program that we teach for the Self Pillar, we have an exercise where we fire the inner critic and hire the cheerleader instead so there is a lot of self-gratitude in that level. Pillar Two is the soul, so really reconnecting to your inner guidance system, which is your soul. Really reconnecting to the knowing, really reconnecting into your intuition, changing operating systems. Moving from the human operating system by thinking 'I question' to 'I know, and I trust' which is the soul's operating system. It's a much more superior operating system because it doesn't have so much angst and is a lot cleaner energy, a lot smoother.

And once you're really embodying the Pillar of the Soul and you're really embodying the Pillar of the Self, the third pillar is your Pillar of Service. Now the Pillar of Service becomes your purpose. But the teachings of my spirit team are 'your pillar of service is your purpose'. Every human being has exactly the same purpose.

When I first heard these teachings from my spirit team, I thought, how could we all have the same purpose? It makes no sense. They went on to say, 'Your purpose is just to be you. There's no one else in the world that can do that.' And then I realised that everybody does have the same purpose. And everybody's purpose is unique because everybody is unique. And so your service to the world is being you, unapologetically you. And that then becomes your purpose.

So my purpose is coaching and teaching. It's what I love. It lights my soul on fire. It makes me feel so alive inside. I adore it. I love seeing the light bulbs switch on for people and their lives changing and improving. It's never going to get old for me. But that is me living my purpose of me being me. That's me indulging 100% in what I love. And as I allow myself to do that fully, then what happens is it becomes a service.

Then once self, soul and service are in place, you can really start your embodiment of the final pillar, which is the embodiment of Source. And you are just an extension of Source energy. So when you embody Source, you're allowing your energy to become so squeaky clean inside that you become like a really crystal clear conduit for what needs to come through you. One of the big things is, I don't really create my programs. My programs come through me like my work comes through me because I embody the pillar of Source.

When you don't like yourself, when you don't feel good about yourself, you think you're an idiot, you call yourself names, you're harsh to yourself, you're literally rejecting Source. I did it when I was feeling that way about myself. I was just praying to Source all the time, 'Please give me more.' I couldn't handle what I already had. I had already been given all the things and I had no appreciation for them.

There I was rejecting Source. Right now, I'm not in rejection of Source. And guess what? Source just keeps showing up more and more because I'm so grateful for everything that Source brings me. Even when Source brings me issues, I know there are opportunities.

The third pillar is all about courage because we're so conditioned and conditioning in itself is a veil that hides the truth. In that conditioning, we're trying so hard to be like someone else or to do it the way 'the gurus told me that you reach the millions'. So in the pillar of service, to be unapologetically you and then to build a business around that quite boldly needs a lot of courage.

It means a lot of going against the status quo. But in doing so, I always think of the Marianne Williamson quote that was made so famous by Nelson Mandela, which is, 'As we let our own light shine, we unconsciously give other people permission to do the same'. I think that's the true service affiliate, allowing yourself to embody who you are, what you are.

The reason they are pillars is because I like to see them as like four corners that hold up a roof as opposed to the rungs on the ladder that you need to climb. All of the pillars are equal to each other, and they're all about embodiment. Each pillar requires a level of mastery and a level of embodiment to hold the energy. And then as you go forward, it's more mastery and more embodiment of each pillar. You go deeper and deeper.

Most of us are trying to build businesses from a place in a space that's unknown. You're about to attempt something new, and your brain goes crazy. But let's look at the stats for a moment. You have 100% track record of getting through life because otherwise you wouldn't be here. What makes you think that your winning streak is suddenly just going to go? Because you've always had 100% track record. And while we're on this subject, money has always been there for you, even when you tell the story that you were stony broke. But you had enough to get to the next day and the day beyond that. And the day beyond that. And here you are today. We're so obsessed with telling stories that aren't even true. And when we start to appreciate the world around us, when we start to appreciate what we have and we start to see, we actually start to see the truth that we've never been without.

We're not dead. We've got 100% track record of getting through life. Can we get some gratitude for that? And can we get some gratitude for the fact that your POW money has shown up enough for you to survive every single day of your life? And you start to realise, actually, I'm really freaking lucky.

It's so simple. It's just putting your hand on your heart, taking a deep breath in and saying, 'I'm going to be okay no matter what,' and really, really deepening into that space inside of you.

It's such a high vibration because of gratitude. Some of my clients take before and after photos of just when they're on a call with me for a session because their whole being changes. They look so different after the call, like they're glowing. And it's not even that they're just smiling on the camera. There's something different in the energy. It's such a difference. And they feel it, too.

Gratitude brings us into a state of Grace.

Veronica Gallipo

'The struggle ends when gratitude begins.'
NEALE DONALD WALSCH

Here I am again, hoping the shower will drown my sounds of overwhelm and heaviness as I beg this feeling to pass. I look through my wet eyelashes and weirdly notice what seems a gentle thread of light directing me down toward my feet, my little feet.

Suddenly, I sense a whisper, a suggestion; they are your pretty petite feet.

My pretty feet? A part of me.

Then more whispers, 'Are you not grateful for your feet?'

Yes, right, they are mine and I should seek respite in something small and pretty much overlooked.

Yes, thank you, feet.

I realise I have taken for granted my feet, my little toes or my ability to walk. But then, something tugs at me, a sense of hope, an understanding that not everything about me is unworthy of love.

Of course, I have appreciated things before, but if I was honest, maybe not in this desperate way. While I was struggling, I felt a lot of me was wrong, that I couldn't do anything right and always wondered what people were thinking about me, all because I felt I was failing as a woman, mum and partner. I share because this was my true journey into understanding the authentic way and power of appreciation.

This literal glimmer of self-beauty awareness helped me on so many levels. Gratitude on this scale yet at the same time so minute was the turning point of realising my worth and appreciating my existence. Yes, truthfully, I couldn't see the light but once taking an aware-filled moment of actually paying attention to my feet, loving my unique soles, allowed me a small window of seeing other things more clearly. That is seeing my life in a whole different way, possibly in a whole other realm. I look now and wonder if finally I was given permission to shift vibration levels or given the key.

Gratitude, I believe from every cell in my body — yes, all the way to my toes — is where healing and growth really occurs. When you begin to embrace, acknowledge, and honestly sit in the sense of humbled gratitude in any tiny possible way, more comes to you.

I can't really explain why that shower moment and many after was the time when my gratitude journals, writing and listing began to take a new turn. After millions of words, I'm sure, and over many years of listing what I was grateful for, I now feel these were more from external surface gratitude, not quite profound and impacting. Today my gratitude references are mixed with vulnerability, feelings and are a genuine acknowledgement of my unique Me-ness. My appreciation grew wings of power and wow, my journey within began to shift, shed and shine. Sadly I was taking for granted many of the true things, overlooking the hidden gifts amongst the cloudy messy spaces that occurred in my life.

Now I am so much more aware and understand the power of noticing the hidden gem in the darkness as often as possible and when I stop and choose to appreciate, I feel true bliss all over.

When people hear I am a Life Coach, I get asked, 'What are your top tips?'

My answer is always:

#1 Love. That is, learning to love, living with love, for yourself and your life and all people and things it entails on a level that resonates. I feel the energy around love is so vital and healing that if we continue to grow and revert to something with a loving collective, then things feel and seem easier to handle and quicker to pass.

Of course, loving ourselves is the essence of a foundation of health, happiness and harmony rippling out to the whole universe.

#2 Change. That is, the incredible power of getting comfortable in the uncomfortable. I always recommend and guide people to try new things and change life up often. Practising change prevents comfort zones from being created, which trap us into false safe, stuck zones, making it harder to cope with change and things occurring that are unwanted or planned. When we allow our minds and bodies to adjust to change, we sit in a powerful responsive place rather than a reactive and disappointed space. Creating a comfort zone in change is where curiosity and wonder sits rather than in habitual living, where we miss so much.

#3 Gratitude. The most important and without hesitation for me is the act of appreciating. Having a conscious awareness of stopping and feeling gratitude in whatever you can as often as possible is where self-empowerment starts. The minute you truly begin to seek and feel the wonders of your life, everything begins to change and is highlighted. You notice more and more comes to you. The abundance we have in ourselves, our environment, the people that surround us, our thoughts, our skills, our belongings; the list is incredible and sadly, a lot is assumed and taken for granted. We sometimes sit in a space where we feel we are owed things or that once we are lucky to attract something or someone in our life, we believe that it is ours forever without humble attention and acknowledgement. Embracing gratitude, making gratitude a daily decision is so vital.

Through my studies, I have learned that gratitude is not just a kind act or a spiritual act alone but a science-based brain, body and life enhancement act. Research has shown the incredible impact gratefulness has on our well-being. Multiple groups in varying ways have been tested, looking at how people are grateful, how people express gratitude internally or shared and what the feelings of being thankful are. Each test showed remarkable results, all different and impactful.

For example, Dopamine and Serotonin levels increase with every soul-full feeling of thankfulness and enrichment for something in our lives or the world. These are sometimes referred to as feel-good brain chemicals, which help us shift our moods to a happier positive place, balancing our bodies and lifting our spirits. Of course, when we are sitting in a position of happiness, it is easier to share this joy without effort. Feeling gratitude increases the desire to give, which raises more feelings of gratitude, allowing an incredible cycle to build and so many things benefit, from our internal state to our surroundings.

Other benefits included better sleep, decreased pain, lower health problems, and increased healing capacity, to name a few; and all of these, as we all know, are beneficial in all areas, most importantly longevity. However, when our life gets so turmoiled in stresses, struggles, and sicknesses, this decreases our capacity to cope and function, making life much harder.

As much as this information regarding the power of thankfulness is expressed in many books and through many professional avenues, I want to say that I am a strong example of how living with gratefulness can change one's life. I spent many years in anxious stress-driven life, where my sleep was affected, my body felt intense pain and ailments too often and my ability to cope was minimal.

One of the most remarkable changes came when I stepped into this self-gratitude space. Changing my perception of myself, considering my worth and finding the unique blessings I brought to the world allowed me to see everything differently. I will be honest, this did not happen easily or overnight and there were other factors such as beliefs and old patterning of how I saw myself and the world. However, this new version of lenses I tapped into within myself and then my surroundings allowed me to have incredible new insights. I noticed how my state of being affected my body, mind, soul and the closest people in my life.

Because when you sit, in 'Oh no', 'It's all too hard', 'I can't do it', you share and spread the same energy unconsciously to those around you. When I felt a glimmer of my worth, realised my attributes, and my worth to this world, those around me and myself, I felt centred; I had more clarity, I made decisions that resonated with my truth rather than scattered and desperate. My life changed on so many levels that I literally did not recognise myself.

When you begin to grasp that this is your one life and you have this choice to live it the way you want, you then step into the most valid form of you. You understand gratitude on an even stronger level again. You don't take things for granted or miss something. Instead, you sit in utter thankfulness. The more you resonate in the feelings of gratitude for your life, little and big things, then you get more to value and appreciate.

During these past years of guiding people on transforming their lives their way, I began to shift myself deeper to a humbler place. Finding this purpose of giving and sharing my learnings through my coaching path has allowed me to sit in an inner peace and flow that has helped me beyond words.

I feel the best way to describe living in gratitude is living with a gracious attitude.

Gracious attitude is when we make a conscious choice of deliberately expressing appreciation: whether through writing, through conversation, in prayer or meditation, out loud to your material possessions, Mother Nature or just with a soul feeling. This is where we honour our life, self, and what we have instead of putting energy into what we lack.

Deciding to look at how we unconsciously express and perceive what we have around us will allow us to have insight into whether we need to choose a different attitude. When we are aware of our patterns with purpose, we can actually choose to view ourselves and life with wonder and awe. With this shift, we create a new set of guidelines in our mind and heart that resonate in abundance and prosperity: not just in a wealth of money but in a wealth of awareness and knowledge in all aspects of our life.

Beginning to choose to shift how we see ourselves, life and the bigger picture with appraisement is when the actual growth of our perception of our life happens. When you have a broad abundant look, view, scenic take on your one life, you are in the energy of being able to be giving more of yourself, receiving more for yourself and moving forward and upward with incredible benefits.

- It is a pastime worth pursuing;
- it is an action worth scheduling;
- it is an act worth mastering;
- it is a natural wonder you can possess for free and guaranteeing extraordinary results.

Through my studies, client sessions and personal experiences, I have found an incredible and profound bonus to seeking gratitude as often as we can and that aids in healing and moving through traumatic episodes we have in life. We have all experienced people, situations, memories and stories that we have held on to and that have created immense sadness, pain and struggle. I want to share the most exquisite hidden genius side of gratitude.

I want to refer to it as the Gems of Gratitude. It is taken from an incredible process that Benjamin Harvey from Authentic Education expertly created. I take my clients through it, often allowing them to move past where they are stuck and move on quicker.

When you find yourself repeating a scenario over and over in your head, holding negative and heavy feelings, it is usually from some deep disappointment you were hoping or expecting. It is our natural state to sit and repeat and feel the same over and over again because the story you have, the belief you hold, serves you in some way. Now, I want to offer you a new view and that's where the power lies, where the healing can begin to occur. Healing is a choice; letting go can be an intense concept, but imagine doing this knowing you will feel lighter and stronger after, allowing you to see benefits in many areas of your life. Consider this as a cleanse, a sort of internal resolve. Here is a simple version of the process that you can begin trialling as soon as you desire.

First, allow yourself some quiet self-reflection time, where there will be no disturbances. Then, have note paper and pen to capture any insights.

Now take a few breaths and relax your mind so you can tap into your feelings and the situation that you have held on to. Then slowly go through your memory of the event, looking from all points of view. Take in what the surroundings are, who are the people, how they feel and what everyone is doing and saying, rather than just from your position.

This new reflection point will allow you to begin to see what you misinterpreted or misunderstood. Then, as you reflect on these new vantage points, you can start to consider what you can appreciate from revisiting your experience this way. For example, you may have found that you realised you didn't stand up for yourself. Therefore the 'Gem' is appreciating your right to voice yourself clearer. You may have realised that the other person was fearful or nervous and got carried away; the 'Gem' is the lesson of being more patient to prevent jumping to conclusions.

Each small awareness is a Gem of knowledge to be seen as something to appreciate. This process is a valuable way to move past old things that keep us stuck. Capturing gratitude on this level totally flipped my attitude about my life. I began to see consciously that each of our lives is precious and to bypass it, assuming it's ours without effort or awareness, is not enough. So I hope by sharing my outlook on gratitude, I have convinced you to step into this gracious way of living.

Gratitude entwined correctly in your life should not be with just a bunch of words but a feeling that will always carry an energy of centred love and authenticity. So please don't take my word, instead, be curious and seek this profoundness for yourself.

Your one life is precious; the way you live it can be with incredibly varied possibilities and how you perceive it is down to you, so choose with intent every day and appreciate with energy and feeling.

Remember, because your empowered gratefulness affects everything in you and around you, I look forward to feeling the resonance of all your wondrous experiences in gratitude throughout the world.

From my heart, I thank you in advance.

Love
Veronica Galipo
Vivid Living Coaching

Kevin Monroe

My gratitude journey started in a really dark place. I know we hear that a lot from people, but there are some dates that stick out vividly in my mind. April 17, 2018 is one of those days. It was one of those really dark days. I've had three real bouts with depression in my adult life that I can really mark. I think I was on the verge of a fourth that day.

I am usually up between 4:30am and 5:00am. Without an alarm clock. That morning, I could not drag my fanny out of bed. At 7:30am I got up, came into my office and this to me is the power of a daily routine. I have a daily routine. I did not feel like doing it that day, but I grabbed my journal and I sat on the floor and I cried out a prayer. I have it in my journal.

Holy Spirit, you are the source of creativity in the universe, spark creativity in me.

And I just shut my book. That was all I could get out that day. And I laid on the floor in that thing I call liminal space. I was probably in and out of sleep. I was in and out of a daze and 45 minutes later I sat up erect and there was an idea that was 85% to 90% fully formed. Launch a 90-day program. Call it the Extraordinary Experiment, because I believe most people on the planet when they look in the mirror, they see what I see when I look in the mirror.

An ordinary guy or an ordinary gal, no exceptional talent or really exceptional desire. From the time I was a teenager, I've known I wanted to make the world a better place. That's just been a desire that has fuelled me all of my life. And it's taken me in a zigzag path with different ways to try to express that. But when I look at myself, I'm just an ordinary guy. But I thought, well, what if we did this? What if we created 13 weekly challenges?

I called my friend Christy and said, 'I've got an idea, what do you think of doing this?' She said, 'I'm in'. We had a landing page set up the next day, we started recruiting and found 274 people from 28 countries who said, 'We're in' and we started this.

The rhythm was that on Mondays, we put out a video. On Wednesdays we sent an email that was some kind of encouragement or some tips, tricks, whatever it was we were focusing on that week. And then on Friday, we just invited people to reflect back. We had a survey tool we used and we asked people to reflect what were their experiences of the week. What did they notice? Week one was just the awareness challenge because most of us live totally self-absorbed, unaware of what's going on around us.

Week six I remember vividly. It was the Gratitude Challenge, and that was the first time in my life that I asked the question, 'Is there something different between being thankful and being grateful?' Because we were putting a video out on Monday and thought, we need to address this. And that was it. That was the first time. Oh, my gosh. And I realised it's different, and we didn't call it the Thankful Challenge. We called it the Gratitude Challenge. So that was where it started for me.

About that same time, maybe a little earlier, I had stumbled on two loops, the 'scarcity loop' and the 'abundance loop' that I had seen in a couple of blog posts and online. I was doing work with the Meals on Wheels of America Group, and I was going to speak at a conference and wanted to use these loops. They said, 'If you're using any copyrighted material, you need to have permission to use it.' So I set out on a quest to find who created these loops. It took me six months and I found that Juliana Park wrote a book called *The Abundance Loop* but it included the scarcity loop.

The scarcity loop is like a clock face with four points. It starts with fear. Fear creates anxiety. Anxiety leads us to make poor choices. Poor choices lead to negative outcomes in life. And that's the scarcity loop. And I think everybody recognises it when we see it. We don't realise it when we're in it.

When we're in, it's like a sucking vortex. It's just pulling us down. We're going further and further down, like water down the drain, and the abundance loop has the opposite effect. It took Juliana a year to develop these two loops because she was living this, trying to figure out why she was having negative outcomes in her life, so she found them backwards. But then she presents them forwards. The abundance loop starts with gratitude. Now I didn't understand this at the time. I knew Elizabeth Kubler-Ross's work that notes there are only two primary emotions, fear and love.

I asked Juliana about that, and she said she wanted to say love, but love is hard for some people to activate or actualise so she landed on gratitude. Now I've learned that gratitude and love resonate at the same frequency, and they are at the highest frequency. So she started with gratitude. Gratitude produces peace of mind. Peace of mind allows us to make wise choices and wise choices produce positive outcomes. So those were the two loops. I was hosting a podcast at the time, and I started asking every guest, 'What are you grateful for in this moment?' We grounded every episode of the podcast with gratitude. In my journey of gratitude, I had a mentor years ago who said, 'Think of three things you're grateful for before your feet hit the floor when you're getting out of bed in the morning.'

When I'm honest about that, I probably only had a list of six or seven things that I recycled through every day. I'm thankful for my family. I'm thankful for our home. I'm thankful for my job. I'm thankful for my wife. I'm thankful for our children, but it was still kind of this short list. About that time I started journaling at least three things a day that I was thankful for. And this morning I listed entry number 5015 on the list. So I just started numbering this list every day, and I don't have a rule against not repeating myself. But I wanted to just go deeper.

And I wanted to what I now call *amp up* my gratitude. Not just say I'm grateful for my wife, but really think about something meaningful with that. What's specific about when am I grateful? So that started this journey, then a year later on June 17, 2019 in that time of the morning prayer meditation, there was this thought, this invitation, I believe, from the universe to host a gratitude challenge.

A friend that was joining me on the podcast had written a book on gratitude. I called him up, said, 'Hey, Steve, what do you think of us hosting a gratitude challenge?' He said, 'Count me in.' I thought he'd push back. I thought he'd have all kinds of objections or questions. How would we do that? So I called Christie again, and the three of us jumped on a Zoom call that afternoon and outlined what we could do.

What's the least amount of time that we could invite people to [undertake] a gratitude challenge and then really see a difference in their life? What's long enough that people would see a difference and short enough that people would complete it? Those were the parameters. We landed on ten days and started a 10-day gratitude challenge. I've now hosted 22 or 23 sessions of that and have had over 2500 people from 53 countries of the world join us in those gratitude challenges, and then it just grew from there.

It just snowballed. On September 10, 2020 I was on my morning walk and up to that time, gratitude had just been this thing I was doing, one of my friends called it a side hustle. But that morning, this question was just there: of all the things that energise and excite you, what is the one thing that has the broadest appeal and the greatest impact? My immediate answer was gratitude. I made a decision that day to host a gratitude encounter on the first Tuesday of the month for the next seven months just to see what would happen. Twelve months later it was still going.

I have no plans of stopping at this point and have even expanded that work. Other things came out of that and I decided to go all in and make gratitude in my life's work.

I was invited to create a 30-day challenge and so I pondered what to do. We had been running these 10-day challenges so I landed on that. I wanted to do it on gratitude because that was where I was focusing all of my work. We called it 30 days in the Power of Gratitude and the name kind of came through inspiration. Some of the most amazing things happened.

In our last journey, we were doing our celebration session, and there was a young woman called April. And she'd been very clear about this in the journey that she struggled with anxiety, anxiety attacks, panic attacks. In our celebration session, I use a tool called Minty metre, and we ask questions and populate word clouds. And I asked the question, what word or phrase would you use to describe your experience of this 30-day journey in the Power of Gratitude. I saw a word on the screen I'd never seen before: tranquillity. And I asked who wrote it.

April said she did and was willing to share more about it. 'You all know I have panic attacks,' she said. 'I didn't have a single attack and I wasn't paralysed by anxiety. For 30 days, I experienced tranquillity.'

I felt a nudge, and I was uncomfortable but I asked, 'How often do you go 30 days without this terror, this panic, these attacks?'

'Never,' she said. 'I've never done it before.'

That's the power of gratitude. Another guy on day 28 posted, 'For the past five years, I've been taking antidepressants. Over the past year and a half I've done a lot of work, counselling, prayer, even relocated my family, simplified my life and with this 30-day challenge being the icing on the cake. I talked to my doctor today about getting off antidepressants, and we developed a 30-day plan for me to get off medication.'

So I love that we called it the power of gratitude because that's what people are encountering.

There's this shift that happens. The other thing that amazes me, there are five or six people that have been through all five sessions of this 30 days in the power of gratitude with me. And I always joke, 'It's not because they're slow learners, right?' They realise that they go deeper every time, that the experience is different, that it's richer, that it's more robust. And again, that's amazing as well. There's just so much depth that we tap into through gratitude.

I host these gratitude encounters that I was talking about and every time we have people who are joining for the first time, we have people who know no one else in the Zoom room.

They come in and there's something about the environment that we create. It attracts remarkable people. People come in that are strangers and they lower their guard, they open up to vulnerability, they share things they didn't think they'd share with other people. And I love it when we ask that question, *what word or phrase would you use to describe your experience of this hour together?* And people say *deep connection... rich conversation... authentic... inspiring... Wow, we arrived as strangers, left as friends.*

That's my gratitude journey and it just grows. It's deeper. It's richer.

Tracey Regan

An Attitude Of Gratitude Can Change The Way You See The World

It seems that 'gratitude' is quite the buzz word right now.

Everywhere we turn on Social Media we are being asked what we are grateful for, and then being told no matter how bad things get we can 'all be grateful for something'. There's an implication that there is 'always someone worse off than you!'

The trouble is though, when someone is going through difficult times, and nothing seems to be going right in their life, being told to 'be grateful for what you have' can not only feel condescending, but be extremely difficult to achieve. A pattern of negative thinking takes over and you really have to work at feeling thankful.

But what does it mean to be truly grateful? And is being grateful for 'something' different than practising gratitude every day? I think so!

I've had the opportunity to be 'truly grateful' several times in my life, but most significantly, when someone saved my life!

It was 1990 and I was on a trek in the 'golden triangle' jungle of northern Thailand. We were three days into the trek and had some amazing experiences; swimming in waterfalls, walking by endless fields of beautiful flowering poppies, staying overnight with hill tribes, 'showering' in the torrential rain that seemed to happen at four every afternoon, burning off leeches as big as our little fingers, digging holes to go to the toilet … that sort of thing!

On our last day, we were preparing to raft for four hours down the river, our belongings stuffed into big water-tight drums as the bamboo rafts, although floating, were already ankle-deep in water. And despite the thought of more leeches, we were all barefoot. You may not know, but bamboo is pretty strong stuff and very sharp, and when it's decaying in water it can start to 'peel'. Trust me to be the one to cut my toe stepping onto the raft. The problem was, it was my big toe, and I didn't just cut it, I completely sliced off the whole fleshy underside of my toe about 3mm under the nail.

As the river began to turn red very quickly, I lifted my foot out of the water and realised that the blood was 'spraying' with my heartbeat. I was losing blood at an incredible rate and I have honestly never seen so much blood in my life. It didn't take long for me to realise: 1. We were in the jungle; 2. Any civilisation, i.e. medical care, was more than four hours' 'trek' away; 3. The blood was leaving my body at a very significant flow rate.

I remember one of our group, who had medical training, shoulder lifting me off the raft so I could get to the bank, elevate my foot and apply some pressure. He was using his T-shirt to try and stop the bleeding, but I can still see the look of terror on his face as he realised that trying to stem the blood-flow was almost futile.

Enter my hero! One of the local tour guides, on seeing what happened had run off into the jungle, and as he came running back, was chewing a mass of grey 'gunk' in his mouth. As he reached me, he pulled the wad of chewed up plant (I found out later) from his mouth, and wrapped it around my toe. By this time I was very weak and was told I passed out, but somehow that chewed up plant** did stop the bleeding, and ultimately saved my life.

I still had to travel with the group as there was no other

way out, and no mobiles to call in help, so I spent the rest of the day with my foot up, lying on the raft; there was just no other way out of the jungle. When we got back to town, I was sent straight to the doctor who bandaged me up and gave me some medicine that turned my pee illuminous red for six weeks!

It took months to heal, and 18 months later I had to have an operation to remove the seed pod that had begun to grow in my toe. Yes, I had a plant growing in my body! And wow, am I grateful for the knowledge of the young man who saved my life.

So you see, that really was a moment to be truly grateful for. I'm sure if you think about it, you will be able to list many moments in your life for which you can feel immense gratitude; the birth of a healthy child after a difficult labour, for example, was something for which I will be eternally grateful.

But let's talk more about the 'practice' of gratitude.

It was 2014, so not that long ago, when I first began my 'daily' (not always!) practice of gratitude. I had travelled to the wonderful city of Kuala Lumpur with a friend and business associate to attend a business development course. The course not only focused on business, but also on personal development; the subconscious reasons why we repeat 90% of our behaviours every day without knowing it, and how our cultural programming and limiting beliefs have such an impact on our everyday choices and decisions. I took many wonderful learnings from that course, but one of the things that truly changed my life was that I began a daily journal to record my thoughts and feelings, highs and lows, and part of that was to list three to five things I am grateful for each day.

Anything new that you add to or change in your life takes

a choice — a commitment — but once you have established a routine it takes 30 days to create a habit and becomes so much easier to incorporate into your life. Now I'm not saying that I have written a journal or practised gratitude for every single day of the past six years, but it is definitely part of my life and I find that I am consistently noticing new and amazing things to be thankful for.

And when I went through one of the lowest points in my life, being grateful for what I had learned and experienced really helped me through it.

I was 'madly in love', or so I thought! I was in a relationship with someone I expected to spend the rest of my life with. We had been business associates who lost touch a couple of years prior, but even when I first met him, I had felt a real connection and attraction. We met again by chance in 2015 and his circumstances had changed, he was no longer married, and I couldn't help but act on the attraction. We began dating and had a whirlwind romance. When he told me he loved me, I was stunned. I didn't say I loved him straight away, I actually asked him why he loved me. Until that point, I'd never had someone treat me the way he did in a relationship. However, very early on my sister could see some warning signs. She believed he was controlling, even manipulating, but my rose-coloured glasses wouldn't allow me to see that… at the time. I surrendered and allowed myself to fully feel the all-encompassing emotions.

The first year with him was one of the best years of my life. We had so much fun; travelling, dining out, and he loved to take me dancing and doing adventurous things. Everyone commented on how happy I was, and I was living an amazing life. It seemed that he knew me inside out, and said all the right things to keep me happy. We weren't living together, because I still had a young daughter at home with me, but we talked constantly about our future, where we would live and the amazing places we would travel.

What I didn't know though, was that it was a very different story to his friends. He was only showing me one side of himself. He had a lot of female friends that he liked to catch up with regularly. It wasn't a problem for me, I had no reason not to trust him, and to be fair, they were just friends. But what I found out later, was that he loved to tell stories. He would talk to his girlfriends about me in a very negative way, and sometimes even make up stories about me. Some of his friends became my friends too, and on occasion I would feel like they were a little cold toward me. I found out later that was because he'd told them some intimate, but misleading parts of our conversations, often with a negative spin on me, or even a completely false story.

It wasn't until the second year in our relationship that things started to get 'strange'. Looking back, I realise I was fully part of the 'story' he had created for our lives. I guess once the glasses of new romance started to fade, I began to question some of the things he said. I am quite a strong, confident person but I realised that I hadn't been being fully true to myself. In the first year, if I doubted some of what he said, or questioned him about his behaviour or opinions, he would gently be able to talk me round to his side of the story, and even if I didn't agree with him, I was convinced that his opinion was fair and just. One time I was offered a job opportunity with a friend and he adamantly told me that he wouldn't accept it. I asked him if he was telling me I wasn't 'allowed' to do it, which ultimately he was, but I still found a way to accept his explanation.

But mid-way through our second year, I began to realise that I really didn't agree with some of his values and I was able to become quite vocal about how I felt, especially when there were so many inconsistencies and holes in what he was telling me. He began to get very defensive and secretive, and his behaviour changed, but I was still 'in love' and found ways to make excuses for the behaviour, not just to myself, but to my family and friends who had noticed that things were changing.

When things came crashing down, it all happened very quickly. My daughter was leaving home to study in the UK, and being that she was only 16 at the time, he believed I was making the wrong decision in allowing her to go, and regularly called me a "terrible mother", without any kids of his own, or any experience in that regard.

Backtracking a bit, when planning for the future, we had decided that we were going to knock down the house I owned to build units together, as it was quite a big block. It wasn't something I could do myself, but together we could have had a fairly profitable partnership. We had already talked to builders and knew what we had to do to get started. When my daughter left, a friend said she was interested in buying my property. When I talked to him about it, his words were, "you know, I'm not sure it's worth the hassle, just sell it!' So I did. Because it was all fairly straight forward, paperwork went through quickly and I had an impending move date with just a few weeks to find somewhere to live.

With my daughter gone, for me there was an expectation that we would move in together, but whenever I tried to talk about it, I was brushed off, in fact any conversation was strained. To be honest, his behaviour at this point was very erratic and confusing. My move date was not far away and still we hadn't talked about my living arrangements. He didn't help me at all with my preparations to move, in fact my neighbours thought we had split because it had been so long since they'd seen him. With just a week before I had to leave my house, I refused to be ignored on the subject any longer, and when I asked him if he could help me organise some space to move some of my furniture into his place, I was told that he needed more time to think about it. I had to be out of my house within a week… what was I to do? I had a friend who had a spare room I could temporarily move into, so I decided that was what I would do.

That's when the fun really started. He insisted that I wasn't allowed to move there, but was still not saying I could move in with him. I told him I needed time to think. He would send me crazy texts, for hours through the night. First accusing me of the most awful things, then telling me how much he loved me. He would phone constantly, be angry and aggressive and threatening, and then burst into tears. There were a number of strange events that occurred in our last two months together, but the last time I saw him, we tried to talk about things, and despite me sitting peacefully on the couch, he told me, very calmly, that my behaviour was threatening and he was scared for his life! He said I needed professional help, and threatened to have me taken away by the mental health team to be sectioned for a few days. He said he knew "the right people' to make it happen! I walked out on him then, and after another night of threatening and frankly crazy texts, I blocked him and never saw him again.

I have to say though, I was totally devastated. Despite all the strange behaviour in the last month of our relationship it felt like my whole future and whoever I was in that time had been swept away. I spent the whole of the following week in bed. But what I did do, was to journal and practise my daily gratitude.

I spent the whole week writing down everything I was thankful for in the relationship and what I had learned. I did allow myself to feel sad (I think that's really important), but I focused on the positives and what I'd taken from our time together and I truly believe my practice of gratitude got me through that time of my life.

Looking back now, three years later, I have no regrets. In fact, I am truly grateful for what he gave me. I learnt for the first time that I was able to give and receive pure LOVE. He opened me up to a whole new perspective on the world, letting down my guarded heart. I live my life differently now, being more honest with myself, and open to vulnerability, and absolutely living in the moment.

If I hadn't been practising gratitude daily and training my mind to see the wonderful things we can be thankful for, maybe I would feel differently. So even when life is at its lowest point, try and find just three things each day to be grateful for, and from my experience, I believe an attitude of gratitude will begin to grow, and you can see your life through new eyes.

** **Eupatorium odoratum**
https://pubmed.ncbi.nlm.nih.gov/1783877/#:~:text=The%20purified%20compound%2C%204'%2C,on%20blood%20clotting%20factor%20activities.

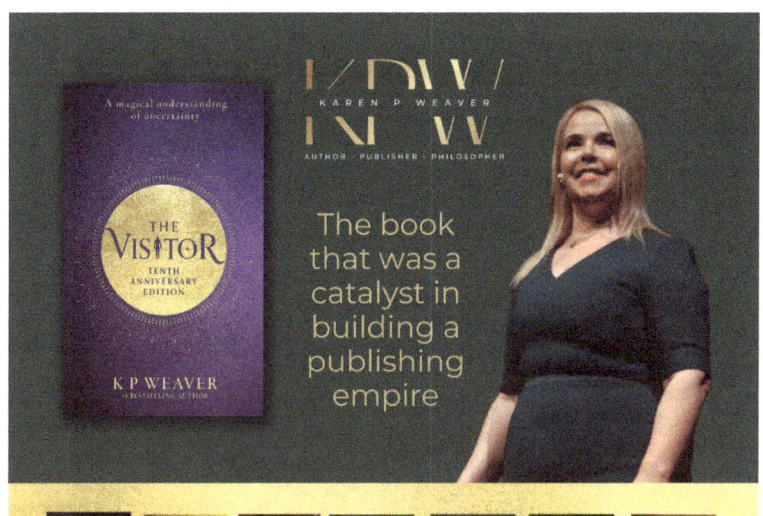

www.ingramcontent.com/pod-product-compliance
Lightning Source LLC
Chambersburg PA
CBHW070729020526
44107CB00077B/2263